STUDIES

IN THE

SOCIAL ASPECTS

OF THE

DEPRESSION

Studies in the Social Aspects of the Depression

Advisory Editor: *ALEX BASKIN*

State University of New York at Stony Brook

RESEARCH MEMORANDUM ON RECREATION IN THE DEPRESSION

By JESSE F. STEINER

ARNO PRESS

A NEW YORK TIMES COMPANY

Reprint Edition 1972 by Arno Press Inc.

Reprinted from a copy in The Newark Public Library

LC# 78-162842
ISBN 0-405-00845-7

Studies in the Social Aspects of the Depression
ISBN for complete set: 0-405-00840-6
See last pages of this volume for titles.

Manufactured in the United States of America

Preface to the New Edition

WHEN THE YOUNG MEN of the Civilian Conservation Corps spread out across the land, they set to work planting trees, reseeding eroded hillsides, repairing forgotten roadways, and building parks, cabins, and campsites. The record of their accomplishments lives in the beautiful stands of tall timber and in the heavily used recreational areas located in many regions in the United States today. In addition to giving meaning to their own lives, the young CCC men provided places where the multitudes who knew the frustration of involuntary unemployment could relax. Men and women with time on their hands needed and wanted escape from their problems and hardships. It is not surprising that athletic programs were popular, that libraries were crowded with readers, that movies became a national pastime, and that radio personalities were known across America. New Deal agencies such as the Works Progress Administration constructed public recreational facilities in local communities that provided baseball diamonds and football fields for youngsters who had previously spent their time dodging traffic on congested city streets. The social and economic significance of the use of leisure time in America in those crucial years is the subject of Jesse F. Steiner's investigation. He examined the consequences of the various efforts made to establish recreational facilities, and their significance as instruments to blunt extremist activities and socially reprehensible acts. His questions about the relationship of the length of hours of labor and the meaningful use of free time continue to concern us for they are still relevant and crucial in our time.

Alex Baskin
Stony Brook, New York, 1971

BULLETIN 32

1937

RESEARCH MEMORANDUM ON RECREATION IN THE DEPRESSION

By JESSE F. STEINER

Professor of Sociology
University of Washington

PREPARED UNDER THE DIRECTION OF THE
COMMITTEE ON STUDIES IN SOCIAL
ASPECTS OF THE DEPRESSION

SOCIAL SCIENCE RESEARCH COUNCIL
230 PARK AVENUE   NEW YORK NY

The Social Science Research Council was organized in 1923 and formally incorporated in 1924, composed of representatives chosen from the seven constituent societies and from time to time from related disciplines such as law, geography, psychiatry, medicine, and others. It is the purpose of the Council to plan, foster, promote, and develop research in the social field.

CONSTITUENT ORGANIZATIONS

American Anthropological Association

American Economic Association

American Historical Association

American Political Science Association

American Psychological Association

American Sociological Society

American Statistical Association

FOREWORD

*By the Committee on Studies in
Social Aspects of the Depression*

THIS monograph on research pertaining to recreation in the depression is one of a series of thirteen sponsored by the Social Science Research Council to stimulate the study of depression effects on various social institutions. The full list of titles is on p. ii.

The depression of the early 1930's was like the explosion of a bomb dropped in the midst of society. All the major social institutions, such as the government, family, church, and school, obviously were profoundly affected and the repercussions were so far reaching that scarcely any type of human activity was untouched. The facts about the impact of the depression on social life, however, have been only partially recorded. It would be valuable to have assembled the vast record of influence of this economic depression on society. Such a record would constitute an especially important preparation for meeting the shock of the next depression, if and when it comes. Theories must be discussed and explored now, if much of the information to test them is not to be lost amid ephemeral sources.

The field is so broad that selection has been necessary. In keeping with its mandate from the Social Science Research Council, the Committee sponsored no studies of an exclusively economic or political nature. The subjects chosen for inclusion were limited in number by resources. The final selection was made by the Committee from a much larger number of proposed subjects, on the basis of social importance and available personnel.

Although the monographs clearly reveal a uniformity of goal, they differ in the manner in which the various authors sought to attain that goal. This is a consequence of the Committee's belief that the promotion of research could best be served by not imposing rigid restrictions on the organization of materials by the contributors. It is felt that the encouraged freedom in approach and organization has resulted in the enrichment of the individual reports and of the series as a whole.

A common goal without rigidity in procedure was secured by requesting each author to examine critically the literature on the depression for the purpose of locating existing data and interpretations already reasonably well established, of discovering the more serious inadequacies in information, and of formulating research problems feasible for study. He was not expected to do this research himself. Nor was he expected to compile a full and systematically treated record of the depression as experienced in his field. Nevertheless, in indicating the new research which is needed, the writers found it necessary to report to some extent on what is known. These volumes actually contain much information on the social influences of the depression, in addition to their analyses of pressing research questions.

The undertaking was under the staff direction of Dr. Samuel A. Stouffer, who worked under the restrictions of a short time limit in order that prompt publication might be assured. He was assisted by Mr. Philip M. Hauser and Mr. A. J. Jaffe. The Committee wishes to express appreciation to the authors, who contributed their time and effort without remuneration, and to the many other individuals who generously lent aid and materials.

William F. Ogburn Chairman
Shelby M. Harrison
Malcolm M. Willey

CONTENTS

Chapter I

Recreational Research: Problems, Trends, Sources

RECREATION as an important field for social research has only recently been given any serious consideration. The wide variety of social and economic problems which engaged the chief attention of research students during the past two decades rarely included recreation and leisure time activities. From time to time attention was called to the growing significance of recreation and leisure in modern life, but those most interested in this field were ordinarily concerned with promotion of recreational facilities rather than with scientific studies. The lack of adequate provision for recreation in an era of rapidly expanding cities stood out as such an obvious and challenging fact that it seemed to call for action rather than for investigation. Public and private agencies were established to meet this need and the available funds as well as the energy of leaders were turned in this direction.

For this reason much of the existing literature in the field of recreation in the period of the depression—as well as pre-depression times—is hortatory, moralistic, descriptive, and popular. The promoter and the administrator, not the research worker, have dominated the scene. Especially voluble have been those concerned with the moral aspects of recreation. Ethical treatises pointing out the demoralizing influence of unwholesome and degrading amusements and urging measures for their control or abolition abound on every hand. Less widespread, but of increasing importance, are the various publications, both governmental and private, concerned with the promotion of public recreation. Government bulletins, reports of planning commissions, and publications of private organizations of various kinds are constantly calling attention to the need of more adequate recreational facilities of a public nature. Much more abundant is the literature that caters to the populace interested in popular recreational activities of various kinds. The sport pages of daily newspapers, the magazines devoted to sports, pleasure travel, and outdoor life in its various forms, are examples of a growing body of writing designed to keep people informed about happenings in the recreational world. The public follows with keen interest the winning of championships, the establishment of new athletic records, achievements of skill and daring, that which is thrilling and sensational in the world of amusements, and the everchanging recreational fads and fashions that make their brief bid for the limelight.

The expansion of literature of these kinds has greatly stimulated popular interest but is utterly inadequate for a systematic analysis of the recreational field. Such items as the records of athletes and championships, attendance at spectacular events, unusual gate receipts, and descriptions of the activities of popular social clubs are of little use to the student interested in factual data showing trends in outdoor recreation, the extent of participation in sports and games, or significant developments in commercial amusements. It has doubtless been this dearth of data available for quantitative and analytical studies that is largely responsible for the failure of universities to give much attention to recreational problems. Courses in recreation and leisure have very slowly found entrance into college curricula and only recently have suitable textbooks begun to appear. Graduate theses rarely dealt with this subject and slow progress was made in accumulating the materials necessary for serious study. A generation ago when the modern recreation movement had its first beginnings, the scholars interested in this field devoted themselves to a discussion of the philosophy and psychology of play.[1] Only gradually did concrete studies appear in the field of recreation itself, and these usually were made in connection with local social surveys which included a chapter dealing with the relation between delinquency and the lack of wholesome leisure time activities. It has only been since the World War that detailed recreational surveys of urban communities have become more common, and the first study attempting to determine recent trends in recreation for the entire country was not published until 1932.[2]

In spite, however, of the slow progress of research in this field, serious and authoritative studies of various aspects of recreation have been made and are rapidly increasing in number. The recent emphasis upon better planning for the recreation of the future makes very timely this expanding interest in research in this field. Varied ways of dealing with our recreational problems are constantly being proposed and there is urgently needed a sounder factual basis upon which to form judgments concerning the validity of the specific programs that are clamoring for public support. At this particular time as we emerge from the years of the financial depression, it is especially important that we study critically the developments in the recreational world during this difficult period when expenditures were so sharply curtailed. One of our most perplexing problems, for example, is how to avoid continuously mounting costs in the field of recreation as leisure expands and becomes more widely distributed among all classes of people. In dealing with this problem the experience gained during hard times may indicate how recreational needs can be satisfied most economically, thus pointing the way to less extravagant expenditures in

---

[1] Groos, Karl. *The Play of Man.* New York: D. Appleton and Co. 1898; Patrick, G. T. W. *The Psychology of Relaxation.* Boston: Houghton Mifflin Co. 1916

[2] *Recent Social Trends.* New York: McGraw-Hill Book Co. 1933 II, Chapter XVIII

the future. In the past there has been no widespread effort to plan adequately for the best utilization of leisure. Certain groups, some impelled by civic and humanitarian purposes and others concerned merely with private pleasure or profit, have promoted programs with varying degrees of success. Before comprehensive recreational planning can become possible, there must be available studies that illumine the values of past experience and set forth full knowledge of existing conditions. Already an excellent beginning has been made in recreational research of this kind, but more extended studies are needed. Recreation and leisure, as fields for research, offer especially fruitful opportunities to students interested in topics that have not yet been widely exploited.

The student who undertakes research in the field of recreation faces serious difficulties growing out of the nature of his source materials. Not merely is the information at his disposal scattered and fragmentary, but much of it is too general to be satisfactory for his purpose. A great deal of the official data concerning recreation in government reports is of little value to the student through failure to assemble or present it in sufficient detail. A further difficulty arises from the tendency even in official publications to publish fragmentary or estimated figures which later come to be accepted as reliable totals. Although attention may be called in the original text or in footnotes to the shortcomings of these figures, these words of caution are easily overlooked or forgotten with the result that the data may be widely quoted as authoritative statements of fact. The inaccuracies growing out of this careless use of data are especially noticeable in published statements covering the cost of recreation. A problem of another kind arises because of different methods of counting attendance, as for example at public parks, and the lack of standardized forms in reporting recreation statistics. No one has been able as yet to find a satisfactory solution for uniform report-keeping in this field. One child may be on a playground for only a period of ten or fifteen minutes during the day; another may be there for practically the entire time that the playground is open; while still another child may be in and out for short intervals during the day. There is room for the application of ingenuity in determining how such attendance can be counted. A brief analysis of some of the types of source materials available for students of recreation and leisure will make clear both the possibilities and limitations of research in this field.

Of great importance is the wide variety of government reports and publications from which may be gleaned recreational data of different kinds. Among these may be listed first the census volumes that need to be consulted. From the biennial Census of Manufactures there can be secured information concerning changes in the production of sporting goods. In the 1929 and 1931 publications, the different kinds of sporting goods were reported upon separately both as to quantity and value, thus making it possible to determine changes in the use of equipment for various sports and games. Unfortunately, the later reports issued during the depression were so greatly abbreviated that they are useful only in ascertaining trends in a most general way. For example, a comparison of the 1929 and 1931 reports shows that while the value of footballs manufactured during those years declined 6 per cent, their actual number almost doubled. Baseball equipment showed a similar decrease in value with an increase in the number of balls and bats manufactured. The failure of the 1933 and 1935 reports to publish detailed figures covering quantity as well as value makes it impossible to determine whether the decline in the sporting goods industry during the depression was due to lowered prices or to actual reduction in the quantity of goods manufactured.

The Census of Distribution (retail trade, 1929) reports the number of establishments and net sales of sporting goods stores classified in three groups. Since a very considerable part of the sales of recreational supplies takes place in general stores where the sales of such materials are not reported separately, the census report cannot be used to determine the total sales of sporting goods through retail channels. The Census of American Business (retail distribution, 1933, 1935) does not report sporting goods separately, and consequently no measure can be obtained of the effect of the depression upon retail sales of recreational equipment. The Census of American Business (wholesale distribution, 1933, 1935) gives data on number of establishments and net sales of amusement and sporting goods classified as follows: (a) cameras and motion picture equipment (b) moving picture films (c) sporting goods (general line) (d) toys, novelties, and fireworks (e) all other. The general tables include the figures collected by the Census of Distribution (wholesale trade, 1929), and therefore studies can easily be made of the changes during the depression in the sale of recreational supplies by wholesale houses.

The Census of American Business, 1933, includes a division called *Services, Amusements, and Hotels,* which was the first nationwide census of places of amusement. The types of amusement places covered in this census were amusement parks, athletic fields, bathing beaches, billiard and pool parlors and bowling alleys, dance halls, skating rinks, theaters, boats and canoe hiring concessions, boxing and wrestling arenas, carnivals, private museums, observation floors and towers, race tracks, riding academies, rodeos, shooting galleries, circuses, dance marathons, etc. In the published tables, these commercial amusements are classified into five groups as follows: (1) billiard and pool parlors and bowling alleys (2) dance halls (3) skating rinks (4) theaters (legitimate stage and motion picture theaters reported separately) (5) other amusements. The information given includes the number of establishments, receipts, admissions, and per capita expenditures, all being reported for each state, county, and city. The tables are based upon a field canvass made during 1934 and are perhaps incomplete for establishments of a seasonal character which were closed at the time of the census. This material on commercial amusements, together with similar data included in the 1935 Census of American Business, comprise our most valuable data concerning this field of recreation. The division of this same census dealing with hotels reports separately seasonal hotels which rely principally upon tourist trade. These 1933 figures on hotels can be compared with similar data reported in the 1930 decennial census, although the latter omitted hotels having less than 25 guest rooms. It is unfortunate that the 1933 hotel census was taken at a time of year when many of the seasonal hotels were closed.

Other recreational data of importance are found in the annual volumes issued by the Bureau of the Census entitled the *Financial Statistics of Cities* and the *Financial Statistics of States*. From the first named volume information can be secured concerning the total and per capita cost and the percentage distribution of payments for the operation and maintenance of departments of recreation and other city departments, in cities of 30,000 population or more. This is reported for cities of the different population classes as well as for individual cities. All forms of recreation such as parks, golf courses, museums, zoölogical gardens, etc., are grouped together instead of being reported upon separately. The volume entitled *Financial Statistics of States* reports in a similar way the recreational .expenditures of the various states. In the interests of economy the annual publication of this latter volume was discontinued between the fiscal years 1933 and 1935 and the *Financial Statistics of Cities* during this period was limited to data from cities of 100,000 population or more, thus greatly decreasing the usefulness of these sources in a study of the depression. There should be mentioned also the decennial census volume for the year 1932 called the *Financial Statistics of States and Local Governments,* which contains data on recreational expenditures for that year.

In addition to the information available in publications of the Bureau of the Census, other important source materials can be found in various reports and bulletins issued by federal departments and bureaus. Especially useful in studies of outdoor recreation are the annual reports of the National Park Service and the National Forest Service, which for a number of years have provided detailed information concerning the number of visitors to these public lands and the activities in which they participate. The annual reports of the Commissioner of Internal Revenue include tables recording the amount of federal taxes paid by social and athletic clubs, pool and billiard parlors, cabarets and road houses, theaters, concert halls, and boxing contests. The chief difficulty in the use of these figures as a measure of recent trends in the field of recreation is the change in the revenue laws in 1933, which not merely increased the tax rates but greatly enlarged the scope of their operation. These reports are also unsatisfactory to the student of recreation because widely different forms of commercial amusements are included in a single classification and no information is given concerning the number of establishments from which taxes are collected.

From the U. S. Bureau of Navigation the number of registered motor and sail boats more than 16 feet in length can be secured but no attempt is made to classify separately those used for pleasure purposes. The number of fishing licenses issued each year by the various states is reported by the U. S. Bureau of Fisheries and similar information concerning hunting licenses can be obtained from the U. S. Bureau of Biological Survey. Detailed estimates of the expenditures of American tourists abroad are published in *The Balance of International Payments of the United States,* an annual bulletin published by the Department of Commerce. These annual estimates are carefully made and are of great assistance in measuring trends in pleasure travel to foreign countries. The expenditures of the federal government by its various bureaus and departments for recreation can be computed, although with considerable difficulty, from the *Combined Statement of Receipts and Expenditures, Balances, etc., of the U. S.,* a publication issued annually by the U. S. Treasury Department.

From the volumes entitled *Foreign Commerce and Navigation of the U. S.,* published by the Department of Commerce, data can be obtained concerning the total value of imports and exports of sporting goods each year. The usefulness of these figures is limited by the failure to list separately the different kinds of sporting goods. From time to time the Department of Labor issues reports and bulletins dealing with industrial welfare activities and the Bureau of Labor Statistics has published within recent years two important studies of municipal park acreage. The Office of Education published as late as 1930 studies of school playgrounds and public school recreation, but this part of their research work was discontinued during the depression. The research divisions of the Federal Emergency Relief Administration and the Works Progress Administration sponsored a considerable number of recreational studies which throw a great deal of light on recreational developments during the past few years. Of great value also are the first reports issued by the National Resources Board which include careful studies of recreational land requirements for the whole nation.

Other governmental publications that should be consulted are annual reports of State Racing Commissions and State Athletic Commissions, which provide data concerning horse racing and professional boxing and wrestling contests. Where state park commissions have been established, important information about the development of state parks can be gained from their annual reports. Reports of municipal and county park departments and recreation commissions are frequently very elaborate but are limited in their usefulness to research students because of the lack of standardization in their statistical tables. The wide variations in methods of reporting park attendance and participation in activities make it necessary to use this material with a great deal of caution. The reports issued by the Dominion Bureau of Statistics of the Department of Trade and Commerce of Canada record the number of permits for touring purposes given to United States visitors to Canada and are therefore useful in studies of pleasure travel.

When we turn from government publications to those issued under private auspices, a wide variety of materials is found with varying degrees of usefulness to the research student. The records and reports of national organizations that fall either directly or indirectly in the field of recreation and leisure vary widely in scope and purpose, but on the whole are important sources of information. The National Recreation Association, which is the leading organization in public recreation, publishes annually a yearbook containing a summary of the public recreational activities in all the American cities from which reports can be secured. Variations in the method of presentation and the failure of some cities to make regular and complete reports limit the usefulness of these yearbooks, but they still remain the most valuable source in the field they cover. This organization also publishes from time to time reports of special studies undertaken by its staff members. Its official organ, *Recreation,* contains many items of interest to the student of public recreation.

In the field of private recreation, each sport is represented by a national organization which in some cases has a paid staff and official publications. The United States Golf Association is an excellent example of the more active organizations of this kind. The failure, however, of all golf clubs to become members of this national organization makes it impossible to secure from its reports full data concerning the development of golf facilities in this country. The same thing is true of the United States Lawn Tennis Association, which is primarily interested in the activities of its member clubs and in the promotion and regulation of tournaments held under its auspices. This organization makes no effort to secure information concerning the growing popularity of this game in public park systems, schools, and colleges, summer resorts, and private clubs operating independently. The many national organizations concerned with either specific or general fields of sport are primarily interested in standardizing conditions of competitive play and in keeping records of tournaments and championships. Nevertheless, they constitute a centralized source of information which must not be overlooked by the research student.

Other types of national organizations from which recreational information can be secured are the American Legion, which in recent years has sponsored the Junior National Baseball Championship; the American Automobile Association, whose research division publishes estimates of motor tours and pleasure travel; the National Education Association, with its interest in school community centers and the leisure time activities of school children; the Carnegie Foundation for the Advancement of Teaching, which has issued valuable reports concerning college athletics; The National Collegiate Athletic Association, whose annual reports deal with problems of athletics in American colleges and universities. The American and National Baseball Leagues and the National Association of Baseball Leagues keep records of attendance and receipts at professional games. Annual reports of the National Association of Motion Picture Producers and Distributors of America give information about the progress of the moving picture industry. The Merchants' Association of New York has for years maintained an interest in the daylight saving movement and publishes each year data concerning its progress. The Youth Service Associations such as the Y M C A, Y W C A, Boy Scouts, Girl Scouts, Camp Fire Girls, etc., publish reports of their leisure time programs and activities. Information about the increase of leisure for working people can be obtained from studies issued under the auspices of the National Bureau of Economic Research, the National Industrial

Conference Board, and from reports and bulletins published by the Department of Labor. For studies of that large and varied group of associations which attempt to organize leisure for a serious purpose, attention can most profitably be directed to those that are nationally organized or have built up wide-reaching federations with centralized headquarters and well established publications from which data can be secured. Among such organizations are fraternal orders, luncheon clubs, labor organizations, religious associations, etc.

Yearbooks in the field of sport are not numerous but are very useful when available. Examples are Fraser's *International Golf Year Book* and the *Golfer's Year Book,* both of which provide a fairly complete list of American golf courses with the number of members of private golf clubs. Frank Menke's *All Sports Record Book* has been published annually since 1930 and contains in addition to the usual data on championship records, a considerable amount of material concerning the history and progress of different fields of sport. Trade and business journals interested in the sale and production of sporting goods and playground equipment occasionally publish data of value to the student. A notable example is *Golfdom,* a business journal in the field of golf, which conducts an annual survey of golf clubs and occasionally publishes articles dealing with the expansion of golf facilities in this country.

In addition to these general sources of information, there are available an increasing number of recreational surveys of local communities and other studies of specific aspects of recreation problems. Representative surveys of recreational facilities in cities include among others, the *Cleveland Recreational Survey* (1920); the *Recreation Survey of Buffalo* (1925); *Survey of Recreational Facilities of Rochester, N.Y.* (1929); *Public Recreation: A Study of Parks, Playgrounds, and Other Outdoor Recreation Facilities* (volume 5 of the report of the Committee on a Regional Plan of New York and Environs (1927); *The*

*Leisure of a People: A Report of a Recreational Survey of In-
dianapolis* (1929) ; and *Recreation Survey of St. Paul, Minnesota*
(1934). Examples of intensive studies of leisure time devices and
institutions are *The Taxi Dance Hall* (Chicago, 1932) ; *The Public Dance Hall* (U. S. Department of Labor, 1929) ; *Community
Uses of Schools* (Baltimore, 1927) ; *Parks: A Manual of Municipal and County Parks* (New York, 1929) ; and the Payne
Fund studies of *Motion Pictures and Youth,* a series of 14 monographs showing the influence of moving pictures upon children
and especially their bearing upon conduct. During the past few
years a great deal of local data in the general field of recreation
has been collected and issued in the form of graduate theses by
students in departments of sociology and physical education of
universities. The student interested in compiling a list of published materials in recreation and leisure should consult the bib-
liographies issued from time to time by the Russell Sage Foundation Library and the Library of Congress.

The above-mentioned publications make clear the general nature and wide variety of sources of information at the disposal
of those interested in recreational research. The difficulty of locating all available materials and the vast differences in their
worth and reliability make it essential for the student to be re-
sourceful in his search for data and skillful in his appraisal of
their value. Especially is there danger of mistaken conclusions
growing out of reliance upon types of data that are most easily
accessible. Great care must be taken in the selection and evalu-
ation of data in order to avoid serious errors in conclusions
reached.

A most perplexing problem confronting the student engaged
in recreational research is the selection of types of studies that
will present a well rounded and well balanced picture of leisure
time habits and activities. The fields of recreation are so broad
and the range of activities so extensive that the mere bringing together of the essential facts is a colossal task. The ways in which

leisure is spent vary widely for different groupings of the population, and it is therefore necessary to control, so far as possible, such variables as age, sex, occupation, economic status, education, vigor, physical environment, and local customs or traditions. Comprehensive studies in which all of these characteristics would be considered are likely to be prohibitively expensive. Consequently the research student seems compelled to rely upon segmental studies limited to specific localities, groups, and activities. Such studies, if well conducted and fairly representative of specific population groupings, may in time permit generalizations applicable to the whole situation.

Segmental studies dealing with special types or aspects of recreation usually emphasize activities that are spectacular or popular, and are largely limited to fields where data can be most readily found and assembled. Leisure time activities and diversions provided by commercial interests, private organizations, and under governmental auspices necessitate administrative activities and inevitably become matters of public record, thus accumulating materials of value to the student. Moreover, modern recreation has made its most significant advances in organized and formal activities, and it is these that arouse public interest and become the chief measure of its progress. Recreational research tends therefore to concentrate upon these aspects of recreation with the result that the more informal and individual ways of spending leisure are neglected.

Our lack of accurate knowledge of the interrelations between individual and organized forms of recreation constitutes one of the great gaps in present day recreational research. In our emphasis upon the expansion of the modern recreation movement, little attention has been given to the large proportion of our leisure which still continues to be occupied with many miscellaneous activities of an informal nature. We do not know whether organized recreation has been able to keep pace with the recent increases in the amount of leisure. Studies are not available showing the changing patterns of informal leisure time activities among different types of people. If progress is to be made in this neglected field of study, new sources of information must be uncovered. Among the kinds of data needed are personal records or diaries which describe in sufficient detail the daily round of life during hours of leisure. An important next step in leisure time studies is to devise ways and means of increasing the number of documents of this kind adequately representative of all classes and groups of people. At this stage of development of recreational research, large emphasis must be placed upon field work which includes both careful observation of activities in progress and a wide collection of individual records of ways in which leisure is actually spent.

Chapter II

The Recent Expansion of Leisure

THE more obvious effects of the depression upon recreation and leisure stand out clearly and can be readily stated. Leisure expanded in an unprecedented manner during this period, while recreational activities were seriously curtailed because of lack of funds. The occurrence of either one of these effects alone would have been a matter of major importance with far-reaching implications in the social and economic world. But the expansion of leisure, at a time when people could ill afford to enjoy it, introduced an unusual situation worthy of careful study. The experience gained in dealing with this problem during the period of hard times should be of value in the development of recreational policies in the future.

Leisure in such large measure and so widely distributed among all classes of people is a new experiment in the modern world. Traditionally, leisure was for the favored few and was made possible by the long hours of labor of the many. The gulf between those most fortunately situated and the lower social and economic classes was clearly marked, and the rigid lines of demarcation in the leisure time world of these two groups were looked upon as a matter of course. As the processes of industrialization and urbanization went forward, technological changes brought about shorter hours of labor for the working people and gradually outmoded our earlier conceptions of the proper distribution of leisure. This penetration of democratic principles into the field of leisure represents a distinct break with the past and makes inevitable the development of

16

new recreational patterns comprehensive enough to include all who wish to participate.

The significance of this expanding leisure becomes more clear when we contrast the routine work of the present machine age with the more varied tasks of pioneer days. The struggle for a living in a new country brings adventure and new situations which give zest to life. Working together, in a period when isolation is the common lot of many, becomes a real pleasure, and occasions when all can join in a common task are regarded as recreation of the most highly prized kind. With the development of modern industry and business, routine methods of work reduced to a minimum opportunities to face new situations. As a result of mass production, congestion has supplanted isolation as one of the problems of life. Under these conditions many forms of work tend to become monotonous and hours of labor are endured rather than enjoyed. Constant association with others in daily tasks is looked upon as a matter of course, and no longer does this companionship in work fulfill the function of social intercourse. More and more under modern industrial conditions work and play tend to be widely separated. The modern conception of work for large numbers of people is that it is a task to be completed as expeditiously as possible so that there will be ample time for the enjoyment of leisure.

As a result of this transition from rural to urban conditions of life and work, the whole social and economic order grows in complexity and the struggle for leisure becomes a matter of vital concern. More serious consideration is given to the question as to the proper division of time between work and leisure. What should be the goal of human society in its struggle for leisure? In a reasonably efficient economic system, what proportion of man's time should be required for the production of goods and the performance of life's essential tasks? Must there be wide variations in the hours of labor in different occupations as is now the case? Is the modern trend toward shorter hours imposing a serious financial burden upon business and industry? Can work under modern conditions be made more interesting and attractive so that the pressure for greater leisure will not be so insistent? To what extent can the modern leisure time problem be solved by greater attention to ways and means of decreasing the drudgery and monotony that still make undesirable so many of the tasks of life? In periods of business stagnation is a reduction in working hours a satisfactory method of spreading employment among larger numbers?

These distinctly economic considerations have tended to push into the background the recreational problems that arise as advance is made toward a shorter workday. Has leisure been going forward more rapidly than provisions for enjoying it in a wholesome and constructive manner? Does leisure bring with it hazards against which society must take proper precautions and build up suitable safeguards? Does increased leisure under existing conditions tend to breed discontent rather than make life more satisfying? How great are the inequalities in the amount of leisure in different occupations and economic levels? Did the reduction of hours during the depression tend to reduce these inequalities?

The time is not yet ripe for satisfactory answers to all such questions, but considerable light is thrown upon many of them by an analysis of the movement toward shorter hours during the depression. The long struggle to cut down the length of the workday and the workweek had by the year 1929 achieved considerable success, but it was not until the onset of the recent widespread business stagnation that the movement toward shorter hours gained rapid momentum. A bill limiting working hours to 30 per week under certain conditions was being favorably considered by Congress early in 1933 as a means of dealing with the unemployment emergency, when the passage of the National Recovery Act with its provisions for the limitation of hours under codes of fair competition made unnecessary special legislation concerning hours of labor. Within two years after the establishment of the National Recovery Administration, approximately two-thirds of the workers covered by the industrial codes in operation at that time were enjoying a workweek of forty hours or less. It is estimated that the maximum workweek in 1935 was five hours shorter than in 1929, a reduction in hours far greater than during any similar period in the past.[1]

After the abolition of the NRA in 1935, the demand for a six-hour day and a five-day week again came to the front and has been made a paramount objective by organized labor. The 30-hour week was put into effect by several large employers of labor in spite of the militant opposition of employers' organizations throughout the country to a further shortening of working hours.

The rapidity of this advance in leisure for certain groups of workers has led to extravagant assumptions concerning the extent of the progress made in reducing the hours of labor. Many of the popular statements concerning the challenge of the new leisure seem to assume that the gains in shorter hours during the depression were far more widespread than was actually the case. Accurate generalizations concerning recent reductions in working hours are difficult to make because of the numerous and wide variations in the different trades and occupations as well as in different places. It must also be kept in mind that the basic maximum hours of work may be different from those in actual practice. In many of the codes the arrangements for overtime and other provisions designed to give elasticity to working hours largely nullified the basic agreements concerning the length of the working day. When consideration is given also to the unwillingness of some employers to observe strictly the regulations governing hours of labor, it is quite apparent that even

---

[1] Wolman, Leo. *Wages and Hours under the Codes of Fair Competition.* New York: National Bureau of Economic Research. Bulletin 54. March 15, 1935. P. 8

while the codes were in force, it was easy to overstate the actual gains made in the struggle for shorter hours.

In order to get an adequate picture of the extent of expanding leisure, statements concerning hours of labor in different trades and occupations must be supplemented by figures showing the number of people affected by these variations in the length of time spent on the job. The uneven progress toward the goal of shorter hours is one of the striking facts in the history of the labor movement. The wide publicity given during the depression to the establishment of the 40-hour week led many to accept this as a basic figure for computing the amount of leisure available for the mass of the working people. As a matter of fact, many groups of gainfully employed worked forty hours or less long prior to the depression, while the workweek of thousands of others was not greatly shortened during this period. It is important to know what proportion of the population has actually shared in these advances toward shorter hours. In which industries were the greatest gains made? To what extent were there significant changes in working hours for the millions engaged in public service, in the professions, in business offices, in domestic service, and on farms? More specific studies of the labor situation emphasizing these aspects of the problem must be made before we are in a position to measure with reasonable accuracy our recent progress toward an era of greater leisure.

An appraisal of the actual effects of the depression upon the expansion of leisure is still further complicated by the sudden abolition of the National Recovery Administration in May 1935, which made ineffective the hundreds of codes that had been adopted. With the removal of these governmental restrictions upon the maximum hours of work, it was generally assumed that most of the gains made in the movement for shorter hours would be speedily lost. Extensive studies of this situation have not yet been issued but a preliminary report by the National Industrial Conference Board in January 1936 states that the average hours of work per week in 25 manufacturing industries combined, increased from 36.7 in April 1935 to 38.5 in October of that year or 4.9 per cent. A longer workweek was noted in 18 industries, a shorter workweek in 5 industries, and no change in 2 industries.[2] According to this report a definite increase had taken place in the average workweek but some of the increases could be explained on seasonal grounds. Similar conclusions were reached by the Bureau of Labor Statistics of the Department of Labor. Their findings show that between May and November 1935 there was an average increase of 2 hours in the workweek of manufacturing industries, an increase due mainly to business improvement. Only 2 manufacturing industries—non-ferrous metals and railroad repair shops—were operating as long as 41 hours a week. The lumber and food industries were maintaining 40-hour schedules while all other manufacturing industries were working less than 40 hours a week. Longer hours of work were characteristic of the non-manufacturing industries with the exception of coal mining. Hotel employees had the longest workweek, approximately 48 hours, and electric railway and motor bus operators stood second with 45 hours. In general, however, only slight changes in hours of labor had taken place in the six months following the abolition of the NRA codes.[3]

These findings run counter to statements issued by labor organizations calling attention to the tendency in some lines of work to return to pre-NRA standards. Especially in the service trades and garment-making industries such drastic changes in hours of labor were said to have been made that a return to sweatshop conditions was threatened. No doubt there was a

---

[2] *Wages and Hours Since the Abolition of the NRA.* National Industrial Conference Board Bulletin. January 10, 1936. Vol. 10, No. 1. See also *The Recovery in Wages and Employment.* National Bureau of Economic Research, Bulletin No. 63. December 21, 1936

[3] Boeckel, Richard M. *The Thirty-Hour Week.* Washington: Editorial Research Reports. 1936. 1, No. 3

sufficient number of instances of increased hours to warrant fears of a widespread tendency in this direction. The six-months period reported on in the above-mentioned studies is too short to indicate trends. If business conditions continue to improve, the pressure for longer hours will almost certainly increase. Studies sufficiently detailed to include small establishments as well as large industries must be made from time to time in order that we may know how permanent were the gains in shorter hours brought about during the depression.

This problem is made still more difficult by the inadequacy of statistics of hours of labor to measure the extent of leisure among all the people. Not all have regular employment and vast numbers are not forced to work by the clock. The farmer's work is largely seasonal followed by periods of comparative idleness. The casual and seasonal labor of hundreds of thousands is so irregular that it cannot be accurately measured. The free time of housewives varies widely depending upon labor-saving devices, number and age of children, ability to employ help, etc. Small shopkeepers and professional people in varied lines determine within certain limits their own hours of work. For people falling in these classes it is difficult to compute the amount of their leisure or to determine how much it increased during the depression. The working hours of many of the independently employed must have been cut down during the depression because of the far-reaching effects of the business stagnation. On the other hand, housewives very probably made no gains in leisure. The leisure of children remained largely the same except where the school term was cut down by lack of funds or where children were forced to work because of hard times. In spite of the fact that unemployment involved millions during the past five years, it is probable that at least half of our population did not have their leisure greatly increased by scarcity of employment or by the recent trends toward shorter hours. A thoroughgoing study of leisure time trends must devise ways and means of estimating the extent of leisure among those groups of people whose hours of work or study are too irregular and uncertain to be calculated in the usual manner.

Our inability, however, to measure accurately the increase of leisure during the depression does not obscure the extraordinary trend toward more free time for millions previously accustomed to excessive hours of toil. For the first time in our history vast numbers of wage earners live in a world where they have more time for leisure than they spend in regular employment. Leisure in such full measure has long been available for the fortunate few but not for the rank and file of the people.

This remarkable increase during the past few years in the free time of workers in many trades and occupations has directed public attention to the social significance of widespread leisure. During the earlier years of this movement for shorter hours, it was largely thought of in terms of the efficiency of the workers and the possible effect of shorter hours upon the cost of production and the reduction of unemployment. These economic issues are still being debated vigorously but they no longer dominate the scene alone. As leisure becomes extended more universally, it is more apparent that a new force has been unleashed with power to transform men and build a new social world.

Within the past few years a great deal has been written concerning the effects of expanding leisure upon the mass of the people and its far reaching social implications.[4] In some quarters it is felt that there is a close relation between expanding leisure and the growing restlessness of the people and their discontent with existing social conditions. Leisure gives time for thought, facilitates gatherings for discussion of grievances, and

---

[4] Burns, C. DeLisle. *Leisure in the Modern World.* New York: The Century Co. 1932; Pack, A. N. *The Challenge of Leisure.* New York: The Macmillan Co. 1934; Lundberg, G. A. and Others. *Leisure: A Suburban Study.* New York: Columbia University Press. 1934; Neumeyer, M. H. and E. S. *Leisure and Recreation.* New York: A. S. Barnes and Co. 1936

therefore, it is believed, enhances the danger of social revolt. The old saying that "the devil finds work for idle hands to do" expresses an old suspicion of the evils of leisure, a point of view that still finds place in the thinking of some reactionary groups. On the other hand, it is contended that the wider spread of leisure among the people will result in a social and intellectual advance that will go far toward solving the most pressing problems of the present day.

Much that has been written concerning these problems is purely speculative or impressionistic and reflects little more than the unsupported opinions of the writers. The serious research that has been undertaken is handicapped by the failure of recreational agencies and governmental departments to collect the materials needed in such studies. The kind of data most readily available for the student tells us too little of the daily round of life during leisure hours. The leisure time problem resists analysis because of the multitude of ways in which leisure is spent. Satisfactory appraisals of the effects of expanding leisure upon the American people must be based upon careful studies of the changes in leisure time patterns as hours of work are shortened.

Studies of the expansion of leisure during the depression must deal also with the problem of enforced leisure among the millions of unemployed. Here is an important aspect of the leisure time problem with considerable data available for the research student. The phenomenon of unemployment is of course not new, but never before in our history was it so widespread and devastating in its social and economic effects. Millions habituated to regular hours of labor had to adjust themselves to long periods of idleness with no assurance of satisfactory employment in the future. The leisure that results from such a situation differs radically in quality from that which affords respite from the round of daily toil. The sense of failure, the anxiety for the future, and the feeling of helplessness as savings disappear make inevitable a mental attitude far removed from the exuberant response to normal periods of leisure. How to mitigate the demoralizing effects of leisure forced upon individuals because of inability to find employment has become a major problem.

Significant efforts to deal with this aspect of the unemployment problem were made during the depression through the establishment on an extensive scale of leisure time programs planned specifically for the unemployed. In the attempt to broaden the scope of work relief projects, various types of leisure time activities were sponsored by governmental agencies and were participated in by large numbers of people. These experiments designed to minimize the evils of enforced leisure are of great significance in view of the continued prevalence of unemployment on such a large scale. How successful were these programs? What were the reactions of the unemployed to these efforts of the government to fill their leisure hours with a varied assortment of activities? Did these leisure time programs for the unemployed make their enforced leisure more attractive and thus tend to break down normal desires for employment? The problem of leisure at the present time cannot be limited merely to a consideration of the free time resulting from shorter hours of labor. The constructive use of involuntary leisure is an aspect of the general problem that cannot be ignored. A study of the results of our experience gained during the depression ought to be of great value in working out a proper basis for future action.

The extraordinary emphasis upon leisure, both enforced and voluntary, during the past few years makes this an appropriate time to study the modifications in popular attitudes toward its significance and use. No doubt leisure has greater status than ever before. Its possibilities for both good and evil are more clearly recognized. With all the varied opportunities for the enjoyment of leisure before us we are less inclined to point with pride to achievements made possible by unremitting toil. Our belief in the beneficence of labor does not preclude ample acceptance of the value of leisure.

A study of these changing attitudes is of great importance for they vitally affect both the further struggle for shorter hours of work and the efforts being made to utilize leisure in a more effective manner. To what extent have employers changed their earlier points of view in regard to hours of labor? How widespread is the old belief that leisure for workingmen means demoralizing idleness? Is there evidence that laborers in general regard their new leisure as an opportunity for self-improvement? Are new leisure time habits being developed among different classes of people? As leisure increases, do people give more liberally of their time to civic affairs and public welfare as well as to pleasures and amusements? Are differences between social classes becoming less as leisure becomes more of a common possession shared by all the people? With the development of new techniques for the measurement of social attitudes, studies of the changing attitudes toward leisure and the resulting effects upon leisure time behavior should throw much light on the progress that is being made in adjustment to new conditions.

From this brief review of expanding leisure during the past few years, it is apparent that many of the problems resulting from this advance are far from solution. There are wide gaps in our knowledge of this field which must be filled before we are in a position to begin an effective attack upon these problems. In many cases inadequate records make exceedingly difficult, if not impracticable, reliable answers to questions fundamental to an understanding of the recent growth and distribution of leisure among the different groups of people. Much that has been written concerning hours of labor has been of a partisan nature and therefore cannot always be accepted as an authoritative presentation of objective facts. Moreover, conditions vary so widely in different places and among different social and economic groups that generalizations based upon the limited source materials available must be made with a great deal of caution.

Nevertheless, in spite of these limitations, important additions to our knowledge in this field can be made by carefully planned studies.

The questions raised in the preceding paragraphs are not intended to be all inclusive nor are they arranged in any particular order of importance. They indicate in a general way important lines of research which challenge the best efforts of students concerned with the rapidly emerging problems of leisure. In order to make more clear the specific types of research that fall in this field and the possibility of carrying them through to successful completion, two of the problems previously mentioned have been selected for more detailed suggestions concerning source materials and the methods of attack and procedure that may be followed.

1. *A study of trends in working hours since the abolition of the National Recovery Administration with special emphasis upon the various groups affected by these changes, and the variations in the amount of free time available in the different occupations and professions.* In estimating the extent of leisure time, two factors need to be taken into consideration. One is the amount of added (or lost) leisure time which has accrued to each employed wage earner. How much more time for non-wage earning activities has each employed person gained (or lost) particularly during the depression? The answer to this question would then lead to a determination of the way in which this added leisure time has affected his "normal" daily schedule. The second factor to be considered is the total extent of leisure time for which appropriate leisure time activities must be provided by the community. The important problem that then arises is the extent of the additional burden that falls upon the community or the nation as a whole because of the increased demand for facilities needed for the satisfactory use of leisure.

A beginning can be made in a study of the first of these factors through the use of data made available by M. Ada Beney in the recent publication, *Wages, Hours, and Employment in the United States, 1914-1936*.[5] The author has calculated the actual hours worked per week, per wage earner, by single months from 1920 to the middle of 1936, for all wage earners in manufacturing, for men and women separately, for men skilled and unskilled, and for a large number of various types of manufacturing enterprises. Table I, taken from this volume, sets forth the data concerning the average hours worked per week since 1920, and Table II shows the estimated gain in hours of leisure per wage earner. One of the most noticeable facts is that women gained much less leisure than men, while the skilled male workers (whose hours of work were shorter) gained less than the unskilled.

In order to determine how much leisure was available for all workers in manufacturing enterprises, the data contained in this table must be supplemented by estimates of the total number of employed and unemployed. Since we know the number of hours of leisure gained in, say 1933, multiplying this by the total number employed would give an estimate of the total leisure time available to those working. If we now multiply the length of the workweek in 1920 (which we have here taken as our base) by the number unemployed, we will have an estimate of the total leisure time available to the unemployed. Addition of these two figures would give an estimate of the total amount of leisure time that has to be filled by one leisure time activity or another.

Data on recent changes in the length of the workweek can be obtained from *Wages and Hours Since the Abolition of the NRA* (National Industrial Conference Board Bulletin, Vol. 10, No. 1, January 10, 1936) and Leo Wolman, *The Recovery in Wages and Employment* (National Bureau of Economic Research, Bulletin No. 63, December 21, 1936). Additional data on this subject can also be secured from publications of the

---

[5] Washington, D.C.: National Industrial Conference Board, Study No. 229. 1936

Bureau of Labor Statistics, Brookings Institution, and the American Federation of Labor. The figures given in these studies must, however, be used with a great deal of care. Since complete reports from all manufacturing and other industrial plants cannot be secured, all such figures must be based on samples of

TABLE I

ESTIMATED HOURS WORKED PER WAGE EARNER PER WEEK IN 25 MANUFACTURING INDUSTRIES, BY SEX, AND MALES BY SKILL: UNITED STATES, 1914, 1920–1936[a]

YEAR	TOTAL	MALE	FEMALE	MALE	
				UNSKILLED	SEMI-SKILLED AND SKILLED
1914	51.5	52.2	50.1	52.9	51.7
1920	48.2	49.2	43.0	49.2	49.4
1921	45.6	46.0	43.2	46.5	45.9
1922	49.2	50.0	45.0	50.5	49.8
1923	49.2	50.0	45.0	50.3	49.9
1924	46.9	47.8	42.6	48.9	47.5
1925	48.2	49.0	44.1	50.3	48.6
1926	48.1	49.1	43.5	50.2	48.5
1927	47.7	48.5	43.7	49.9	48.1
1928	47.9	48.8	43.4	50.4	48.5
1929	48.3	49.1	44.2	50.2	48.8
1930	43.9	44.5	40.5	45.9	44.0
1931	40.4	40.4	39.8	41.8	39.7
1932	34.8	34.4	36.3	36.4	35.1
1933	36.4	36.3	36.6	37.4	37.1
1934	34.7	34.8	34.0	34.4	35.0
1935	37.2	37.6	35.2	37.0	37.8
1936[b]	38.9	39.4	35.2	39.1	39.5

[a] Compiled from data in *Wages, Hours, and Employment in the United States, 1914–1936* by M. Ada Beney. National Industrial Conference Board, Study No. 229. 1936

[b] First six months of 1936 only

reporting firms. The question then becomes one of determining the reliability and the representativeness of the sample, and whether or not the changing conditions in these reporting firms can be said to reflect accurately changes in the industry as a whole. In reporting or piecing together a time series, a further precaution must be preserved in that the same establishments must be followed through for the duration of the time series.

These general studies which seek results in terms of averages are of great value but fail to present an adequate picture of the extent of leisure among the large variety of working groups whose employment is irregular or is of such a nature that it cannot readily be included in large scale studies of hours of

TABLE II

ESTIMATED HOURS OF LEISURE GAINED PER WEEK PER WAGE EARNER, SINCE 1920
IN 25 MANUFACTURING INDUSTRIES, BY SEX, AND MALES BY SKILL:
UNITED STATES, 1921–1936[a]

YEAR	TOTAL	MALE	FEMALE	MALE	
				UNSKILLED	SEMI-SKILLED AND SKILLED
1921	2.6	3.2	−.2	2.7	3.5
1922	−1.0	−.8	−2.0	−1.3	−.4
1923	−1.0	−.8	−2.0	−1.1	−.5
1924	1.3	1.4	.4	.3	1.9
1925	0.0	.2	−1.1	−1.1	.8
1926	.1	.1	−.5	−1.0	.9
1927	.5	.7	−.7	−.7	1.3
1928	.3	.4	−.4	−1.2	.9
1929	−.1	.1	−1.2	−1.0	.6
1930	4.3	4.7	2.5	3.3	5.4
1931	7.8	8.8	3.2	7.4	9.7
1932	13.4	14.8	6.7	12.8	14.3
1933	11.8	12.9	6.4	11.8	12.3
1934	13.5	14.4	9.0	14.8	14.4
1935	11.0	11.6	7.8	12.2	11.6
1936	9.3	9.8	7.8	10.1	9.9

[a] Compiled by subtracting the estimated number of hours worked per week in each year from the number of hours worked per week in 1920, for each column in Table I. Minus sign designates loss of leisure, i.e., the lengthening of the working week.

labor. For this reason it is important to supplement these more general statistical studies with detailed analyses of labor groups of all kinds in so far as this may be possible. Because of the magnitude of this task, these studies perhaps should be limited to different types of communities so selected as to be widely representative of the situation as a whole. Through community studies covering industrial and commercial payrolls of all types it should be possible to determine what groups of workers secured how much additional leisure. Unless our knowledge of recent trends in hours of work extends far enough to include all classes of workers, our conclusions about the expansion of leisure will be entirely inadequate.

2. *A study of leisure time programs for the unemployed during the depression.* The important questions to be raised in connection with this topic are the extent to which leisure time programs increased employment, their success in providing relaxation and enjoyment, and their effectiveness in strengthening morale during a period of great discouragement.

In studies dealing with this aspect of leisure time problems it is necessary to rely mainly upon life history and interview materials. Quantitative studies are, however, possible in investigations of leisure time programs as sources of employment. Since private and local governmental budgets for recreation, adult education, and vocational training were on the whole sharply curtailed during the depression period, such studies can profitably be confined to employment opportunities afforded by projects in these fields financed in whole or in part by federal emergency relief and work program funds.

The published and unpublished records of the Civil Works Administration, the Federal Emergency Relief Administration, the Civilian Conservation Corps, the Public Works Administration, the Works Progress Administration, and the permanent government agencies such as the Department of the Interior and the Department of Agriculture,[6] which used emergency funds for the establishment or improvement of parks and forests or other recreational facilities, make possible fairly detailed studies of the number of persons employed, their hours of employment and their earnings. Such data can be obtained from the

---

[6] For list of other agencies, see *Report on Progress of the Works Program,* December 15, 1936. P. 53

federal, regional, state, or local offices of these organizations. The scope of emergency work projects of a recreational or educational character is indicated by the fact that during the month ending April 30, 1936, more than 430,000 persons, whose earnings for that month aggregated about $14,000,000, were employed by the Works Progress Administration alone on projects of this type. Moreover, such studies can include statistical analyses of the number of youths for whom leisure time provision was made by special programs such as that provided by the Civilian Conservation Corps, the Student Aid Program of the Federal Emergency Relief Administration, and the programs of the National Youth Administration.

Studies of the effects of leisure time programs on the unemployed by means of attitude, achievement, or vocational tests could have been carried on most effectively during the height of the depression period. It is now probably too late to secure the most satisfactory results from such studies, since it is necessary to have good control conditions which permit the measurement of the traits desired before and after exposure to specific types of leisure time programs.[7] Nevertheless, in communities where unemployment is still a serious problem, some specific investigations of this type may be possible and fruitful. In the realm of attitudes, for example,[8] studies might be conducted under control conditions of the type referred to in the Peterson-Thurstone study, to gauge the effect of leisure time programs on the attitudes of unemployed persons toward the government, the church, the employer class, their own condition of employment, relief agencies, receiving relief, working on emergency relief programs, etc. It may be possible to arrange for pre-tests of

---

[7] For a good study of changes in attitudes under control conditions, see Peterson, R. C. and Thurstone, L. L. *Motion Pictures and the Social Attitudes of Children.* New York: The Macmillan Co. 1933

[8] For technique of attitude testing see Thurstone, L. L. and Chave, E. J. *The Measurement of Attitudes.* Chicago: University of Chicago Press. 1929

attitudes in adult educational and vocational classes or forums which include large numbers of unemployed, and to compare the results of these pre-tests with tests taken after a series of exposures to such activities. Under similar control conditions it may be possible to employ achievement and vocational tests as well.

On the whole, however, questionnaire and case studies would probably be more fruitful methods for the study of this problem at the present time. Each of these methods makes it possible to examine the experiences of the unemployed through the entire course of the depression, although to be sure it is difficult to control and evaluate properly the factor of memory. Fragmentary and elusive as such studies may be, they would undoubtedly be preferable to no information at all. The insights which they would furnish on the effects of leisure time programs on the persons studied, and on the mechanisms and behavior sequences involved would undoubtedly repay the cost and effort expended.

The following list illustrates the types of questions which should be raised in inquiries of this nature:

1. Does the increase in leisure time due to unemployment result in an increased or decreased expenditure of time by unemployed persons in recreational, educational, or vocational training pursuits? Or does it result in prolonged quests for employment, in providing opportunity for breeding discontent, moroseness, and unhappiness? Does this kind of leisure time actually decrease interest in recreational, educational, or vocational activity?

2. What was the effect of leisure time programs (recreational, educational, vocational, respectively) on unemployed persons:
   a. In providing relaxation and enjoyment;
   b. In creating and changing their attitudes and general outlook;
   c. In strengthening or weakening morale;
   d. In providing for the retention of vocational skills;
   e. In kindling new vocational aims;
   f. In providing opportunities for vocational retraining;
   g. In creating and strengthening interests in educational, artistic, economic, political, international affairs, etc.?

3. What was the influence of leisure time programs on young men and women seeking their first employment?

4. To what extent did these programs make provision for family, group, neighborhood, or community participation in various activities? Did such activities affect the solidarity of familial and group ties and neighborhood and community organization among the unemployed?

Answers or partial answers to these questions and to others of the same character may be available in the case files of local public and private agencies. They may also be obtained through the collection of schedule, interview, or life history materials. In collecting such materials for the study of these types of problems, it is important that adequate controls be established. Data on age, sex, educational achievement, occupation, length of employment, etc. should be obtained and used in selecting and describing the unemployed populations sampled, and the employed populations which, if facilities permit, may be studied as control groups.

A fruitful method of getting light on the effects of unemployment on leisure time activities would be to prepare a schedule listing the more common ways of spending leisure, so arranged that those filling out the schedule could easily indicate the activities at which they spent (1) less time while unemployed, (2) more time while unemployed, and (3) rarely any time whether employed or unemployed. The unemployed to whom this schedule is given should include persons with varying and controlled degrees and types of contact with governmental, private, and commercial types of leisure-time activities. The items in this inquiry might be expanded or contracted so that analysis is possible of activities on a fee or free basis, on the basis of whether they involve active or passive participation, or on a cross classification of these criteria. Such an inquiry might be followed, preferably in a subsequent schedule to the same group, by an inquiry calling for estimates of the amount of time spent at the various activities in some average month of employment or unemployment. An inquiry of this kind would serve as a check on the answers to the first schedule and also should furnish information of value to the student. In order to test the stability and validity of the responses, the inquiry might be repeated to smaller sample groups after the lapse of an adequate period.

The data obtained in response to these schedules can be related to various types of leisure time programs and should furnish some measure of the effects of such programs on the different leisure time activities in which the unemployed engaged. Similar inquiries calling for rank-order arrangements of leisure time activities before, during, and after unemployment on the amount of time spent or on a preference basis may also prove illuminating.

Interview or life history materials should be collected in accordance with well formulated guide questionnaires and outlines which permit the subject to talk or write freely and spontaneously within the areas and sectors of his experience.[9] For example to get at data which might throw light on the morale of unemployed and effect of leisure time activity on morale, one might use the following types of guide questions:

1. What were the problems which troubled you most when you first lost your job? What did you do about them? How did you feel about them?

2. Did these problems clear up or get worse as the length of time which you were unemployed increased? Did any new problems arise as unemployment was prolonged?

3. What or whom did you hold responsible for your predicament when you first lost your job? Describe your thoughts and feelings at that time. Did these change as the length of time which you were unemployed increased? How did these change? What do you think changed them?

4. Describe what you consider to be a typical day during a period in which you were unemployed, indicating roughly the following:

a. The approximate time at which you arose;
b. Approximately when you left the house, if at all;
c. What you did at home and after you left the house;
d. The people you met, if any;
e. The institutions you visited, if any;

---

[9] For a monograph based on this method of research, see Blumer, Herbert. *Movies and Conduct,* New York: The Macmillan Co. 1933

f. What you thought about;

g. How you felt;

h. How you spent the evening.

5. In what kinds of recreational, educational, or vocational activity did you engage while you were unemployed? When you first lost your job? As your length of unemployment increased? Which of these activities did you like best? Which did you spend most time at? Why?

6. How would you compare enjoyment and relaxation you had out of such activities while you were unemployed with what you experienced when you had your job? How do you account for difference, if any?

7. Did you form any new plans or ambitions while you were unemployed? What were they? Were you able to do anything about them? What? How did you get your new plans or ambitions? From what source?

8. What things and persons in your judgment helped the most to keep you in good spirits and helped to keep your courage up while you were unemployed? Describe what you thought and how you felt about these things or persons. How did they help you?

9. Would you say that any recreational, vocational, or educational activities helped you to keep up your spirits or helped to give you courage while you were unemployed? Which ones? Who sponsored them? How did they help you? Describe fully.

The analysis of mass materials of this type will undoubtedly furnish important insights which may be valuable in themselves and which may furnish clues for the formulation of better schedules for quantitative studies. Such data may even make some types of quantitative conclusions possible, although schedule studies will probably prove more efficient and more economical for this purpose.

As indicated above, these brief outlines of possible studies of recent trends in working hours and the effects of leisure time programs for the unemployed serve merely as illustrations of the types of investigations which can be formulated around the problems enumerated in this chapter. There are sufficient data in most local areas for studies of the kinds suggested. Because research in this field is not yet far advanced, skill and ingenuity are essential in planning and conducting such studies, if they are to be carried through in a successful manner.

Chapter III

The Changing Tides of Recreation

NOTHING is more striking than the changes in methods of spending leisure as one generation succeeds another. The middle of the nineteenth century and more especially the close of the Civil War marked the beginning of a new recreational era when the diversions and amusements of provincial America began to give way to athletic sports and games. This new recreational pattern developed at first very slowly and was largely limited to athletic sports as public spectacles. Professionals played the games and the public got its thrill watching from the sidelines the competitive struggle for victory. Not only was it unfashionable for the people to participate actively in athletic sports, but the lack of facilities made it impossible for them to do so. Several decades had to pass by before play began to become popular among the American people. Even as late as 1900 participation in athletic games by adults was largely limited to members of athletic teams and to those who could afford to belong to private athletic or country clubs.

As a result of new inventions and improved standards of living, our recreational habits and attitudes went through a remarkable transformation during the first three decades of the present century. To a greater extent than ever before, recreational devices multiplied manifold, and new fashions in leisure time activities crowded upon one another in bewildering confusion. So widespread was the desire to play that the provision of recreational facilities became a matter of vital public concern. Breaking almost entirely with past traditions, municipal, county, state, and federal governments began spending public money in the promotion of recreation. Private philanthropy widened its traditional field and contributed large sums to provide recreational opportunities for the poor and other disadvantaged classes. The more liberal churches expanded their activities to include leisure time programs. Industry found it advantageous to furnish recreational activities for its employees. Huge business interests multiplied enormously those types of amusement facilities that proved to be commercially profitable. Innumerable groups of people drawn together by a common desire to participate in similar sports and games organized clubs and associations in order to secure for themselves in this cooperative way private facilities for the enjoyment of their leisure.

No phase of American life is more interesting than the rising tide of recreation during the 1920's. It marks the beginning of a new period in which the traditions of rural America gave way to the advance of an urbanized, industrialized world. As cities became crowded and more numerous, people began to turn with new appreciation to the joys of outdoor life. The high tension under which urban people live and work stimulated a growing demand for a large variety of thrilling pleasures. The shortening of the work day brought additional hours of leisure for the enjoyment of recreation. Play for the first time took its place alongside of work and was recognized as one of the major interests of life.

Any attempt to describe the course of development of American recreation in the decade following the World War must lay emphasis upon its universality, its wide diversity of activities, and the tendency toward frequent rather than occasional participation in its enjoyment. Never before did recreation touch so intimately and inevitably the daily lives of the rank and file of the people. No preceding age had such a wide selection of interesting diversions to occupy their leisure. At no previous time was such a large portion of daily leisure spent by the mass of the people in games and diversions of their choice. In spite of the mounting costs of recreation, popular opinion strongly favored the further expansion of recreational opportunities, and there was an insistent demand that expenditures for this purpose should be as ample as economic conditions would permit.

In the midst of this rising tide of recreational development, the financial crash of 1929 came with disconcerting suddenness and produced far-reaching effects. It soon became apparent that the era of extravagance in the pursuit of pleasure had for large numbers of people come at least temporarily to an end. The possibility of bringing expensive sports within reach of the general public was pushed far into the future. Facing the necessity of enforced economy, many people were compelled to reduce drastically their expenditures for recreation. Governmental budgets for the support of public recreation were cut to the bone. This adjustment to a period of financial stringency was inevitable under the circumstances but brought in its train serious problems difficult of solution.

In our efforts to understand the effects of the depression upon the recreational world, consideration must be given to the fact that hard times affected people very unequally. Large numbers were able to live as usual during this period while millions of others were either entirely deprived of their ordinary means of livelihood or found themselves in exceptionally straitened circumstances. Apparently those whose incomes were seriously decreased had to seek forms of recreation within their means while the well-to-do were able to continue to enjoy their accustomed leisure time activities. As a result of this situation, the growing trend toward widespread participation of all economic groups in an increasing variety of recreational pursuits was interrupted, and some of the more highly prized activities, which had seemed within the grasp of the common people, again tended to become symbols of class privilege as was formerly the case.

This closing of the doors of recreation, which had been

opened to such large numbers of people during the 1920's, must have made the pinch of hard times seem more intolerable. Quite probably, no group of American people was willing to accept, even temporarily, a standard of living that did not provide opportunities for the enjoyment of life in hours of leisure. The retrenchments in the field of recreation during the depression tended to widen the gulf between the rich and the poor and was conceivably one factor in the growing discontent among those living on a low economic level. The reaction of American laborers to the limitations imposed upon their recreational life during the past few years is a subject worthy of serious study.

Of interest also was the effect of the depression upon the conspicuous and extravagant recreational expenditures of the wealthy. Many of those who counted their financial losses by the thousands or millions felt compelled to practice economies in their recreational life. For some this meant the sale of expensive yachts, the closing of one or more of their summer or winter estates, the giving up of extended foreign tours, or planning for less expensive vacations. To what extent were the restricted expenditures of this nature sufficient to produce serious economic effects in different fields of labor and make more widespread the effects of the depression? Did the economies of the rich in their enjoyment of leisure materially increase the number of unemployed? Only detailed studies will throw this problem into proper perspective.

It may also be asked whether these enforced changes in the recreational activities of the wealthy increased their fears concerning the security of wealth and made them more determined to fight for their established class privileges. How far is this situation responsible for any trend toward reactionary policies on the part of those who represent vested financial interests? A thorough study of the growing difficulties between capital and labor must take into account recent changes in the recreational worlds of both the rich and the poor in order to understand more fully some of the forces that are strengthening the conflict in the industrial realm.

Among the recent trends in ways of spending leisure, none is more significant than the growing emphasis upon mass recreation. As the demand for interesting and satisfying forms of recreation becomes more insistent and widespread, the spontaneous recreation of intimate groups characteristic of a rural and pioneer people tend to be supplemented, if not supplanted, by forms of recreation that grow out of secondary rather than personal group relationships. In the congested, complex life of cities, the individual and his intimate neighborhood group not merely find it increasingly difficult to carry on the traditional diversions of the past, but it is discovered that through the cooperation of larger groups on a wider scale far more interesting activities become available. Mass recreation, therefore, in its various forms expands rapidly under modern conditions of living and takes on new significance as a means of reaching larger numbers of people.

When leisure expands, as was the case during the depression, mass recreation fills a rôle of unique importance. If the enjoyment of this new leisure is to be brought within reach of the multitude, emphasis must be placed upon forms of diversion that are inexpensive to the individual as well as economical in the use of space. Bathing beaches and public parks where crowds can congregate, grandstands and stadia that facilitate attendance at sports and athletic contests, the motion picture and the radio that bring to millions more attractive entertainment than was formerly available to thousands, fulfill to a remarkable degree these essential conditions for giving recreation greater universality.

During the depression when many had to retrench in their leisure time expenditures, those forms of mass recreation that the individual could enjoy at minimum expense were apparently in great demand. Public parks seemed to enjoy great popularity in spite of lack of funds for proper maintenance. Attendance at motion picture theaters declined, but this form of entertainment continued to be one of America's most popular diversions. The number of families owning radios mounted rapidly between 1930 and 1935. While mass recreation could not escape entirely the devastating effects of the financial stringency, it was quite apparent that this type of leisure time activity was peculiarly appropriate for such an emergency.

In view of the great need for interesting diversions on a wide scale at a low per capita cost, careful studies should be made to determine which types of mass recreation made the most satisfactory adjustments to the difficult financial conditions of the past few years. The experience gained during this period should throw much light on the possibility of meeting the recreational needs of the rank and file of the people with a minimum expenditure of funds. Was there a tendency to exploit unduly the people's desire for entertainment? Were admission prices adjusted to the lowest practicable level or was an effort made to charge all the traffic would bear? What forms of mass recreation were furnished at the lowest per capita cost? As the cost of mass recreation decreases, is there a corresponding decline in quality? Were the types of entertainment within the financial reach of those lowest in the economic scale sufficiently satisfying to attract large numbers of people? Was progress made in popularizing forms of recreation that are comparatively inexpensive? Can any advance be pointed out in making wider and more economical use of the limited play spaces available in the congested portions of cities?

Studies of our experience with mass recreation during the depression will provide basic data of value in planning recreational facilities and programs for the future. In the further development of public recreation we need to know whether there should be greater emphasis upon grandstands, auditoriums, concerts, and entertainments, and similar facilities designed to bring together people en masse during their leisure hours. Perhaps this aspect of the public recreation movement has been neglected because of our interest in developing wider participation in competitive sports and games for those full of youth and vigor. In any event our past policies in building up public recreation should be reviewed in the light of the problems that came to the front in recent years.

Of special interest also is the growth or decline during the depression of those forms of recreation in which the people themselves actively participate. Apparently, the recreational trends during the 1920's pointed in the direction of a fair degree of balance between active and passive leisure time activities. Crowded grandstands and amusement halls had their counterpart in congested bathing beaches and playfields. In a period of financial stringency is this balance between active play and vicarious amusement seriously disturbed?

According to the most accessible evidence, the desire to participate in athletic sports and games did not decline during the depression, although many were forced to give up those sports that were most expensive. The falling off in the number of members of golf clubs, country clubs, and city athletic clubs was widespread, and indicates extensive changes in the recreational activities of many people. It is significant, however, that while private golf clubs lost in membership, municipal golf courses remained crowded as usual. Public tennis courts never lacked for players during the tennis season in spite of the comparatively high cost of equipment needed to play the game. The continued popularity of active recreational activities is seen most fully in the increasingly large use that was made of bathing beaches and swimming pools. The wave of popularity of this type of water sport continued unabated during the depression. In estimated numbers participating it ranks as the most popular American sport. Even in cities where a large portion of the public recreation personnel was dismissed because of lack of funds, life guards at bathing beaches and swimming pools were retained.

The trend toward winter sports, which grew rapidly during the late 1920's, was not turned back by the depression. Ski clubs have sprung up wherever snow makes this sport possible. Skiing is no longer a sport for the hardy few who make spectacular jumps or undertake arduous journeys. Weekend trips to mountains for skiing has recently become a widespread practice indulged in by increasing numbers of people. One-day excursions from Boston and New York into the mountains for winter sports proved to be a profitable undertaking for the railroads during the past few years. In New England winter carnivals have become numerous during the snow season. It was the recent growth of interest in winter sports that is largely responsible for the increased number of visitors to such national parks as Mt. Rainier. Winter sports in national parks have not been promoted by park publicity, but the National Park Service has been compelled to adjust its winter routine to the growing demand for this type of recreation. In so far as funds are available, automobile roads in the parks are now kept open all winter. Of the 24 national parks only 6 are now closed to winter travel. This year round use of the national parks made rapid advances during the depression in spite of the tendency toward a decline in pleasure travel.

However important is evidence of this kind, careful studies of the whole situation must be made before the student is in a position to state reliable conclusions concerning recent trends in this field of recreation.

One approach to this problem is through a study of changes in the demand for equipment in those sports and games in which large numbers of people participate. Of much significance are the great losses suffered by the sporting goods industry during the financial depression. The value of sporting goods produced in this country, as reported by the Census of Manufacture, decreased from $58,289,000 in 1929 to $25,267,000 in 1933, a decline of 57 per cent. According to the Census of Distribution, the net sales of amusement and sporting goods (wholesale trade) declined from $485,400,000 in 1929 to $271,888,000 in 1933, a decline of 44 per cent. This decline in the production and sale of sporting goods points to great economies on the part of players in the purchase and use of equipment. Consideration, however, must be given to such matters as variations in prices from year to year, and the decline or rise of exports and imports of sporting goods, before anything more than the most general conclusions can be drawn from these figures concerning trends in the different fields of sport.

Other types of evidence that bear upon the extent of participation in sports and games during the past few years are the yearbooks of the National Recreation Association, the data available in the files and publications of many national organizations built up in the various fields of sport, the annual reports of federal, state, county, and city parks, and the trade and business journals interested in the sporting goods industry. The bringing together and analysis of the materials of this nature that accumulated from many sources during the depression is an important undertaking in the field of recreational research.

The advancing tide of modern recreation has been characterized by emphasis upon activities that require organization and equipment for their full enjoyment. As urban recreation dominated the scene, the more simple and traditional ways of spending leisure were forced into the background and no longer attracted public attention. With the onset of the depression when modern forms of recreation were seriously restricted through lack of funds, was there a reversal of this trend? When thousands are forced to give up their memberships in clubs and are unable to continue their customary expenditures for commercial recreation, what do they fall back upon for leisure time activities? Was this period of financial stringency characterized by a revival of the more simple and inexpensive amusements and diversions of pioneer days? Did informal visiting and gatherings for friendly conversation increase? Did people in general tend to spend more time in the routine of family life and in the performance of varied tasks about the home?[1] Was there a greater tendency to loaf idly or spend time in unsatisfying activities?

It is obvious that the usual types of studies dealing with expansion in the field of organized recreation throw little light on such questions as these. The fact, for example, that America has approximately two million golfers is impressive when comparison is made with those playing the game 20 years ago. But this advance in golf still involves less than two per cent of our population, and this small proportion of the people spend perhaps no more than one-fifth of their leisure in playing this game. If we were to compute the total time given to sports and games, to commercial amusements, and to the other forms of organized and formal recreation, the free time yet remaining at the disposal of the mass of the people would be surprisingly large. In view of the great expansion of leisure in recent years, the varied activities of modern, organized recreation, at the present time, may bulk no larger in proportion to the total free time consumed than they did before the rise of the modern recreation movement. Unfortunately, little progress has been made in studies of leisure time activities which lie outside the field of modern forms of urban recreation.

During the early stages of the struggle for shorter hours of work when the 10- and 12-hour day was being slowly discarded, the recreational opportunities most eagerly sought were those that provided relaxation and filled the few hours of leisure with pleasurable diversions. With the expansion of leisure to the point where for many the hours of labor occupy less than one-third of the 24-hour day, the earlier attitudes toward leisure time activities need to be adjusted to the new situation. If expanding

---

[1] Cf. Stouffer, Samuel A. and Lazarsfeld, Paul F. *Research Memorandum on the Family in the Depression.* (monograph in this series)

leisure means simply more time for amusements, sports, or aimless activities, its further advance may prove to be more of a liability than an asset. As amount of free time increases, it is reasonable to expect that a fair proportion would be spent constructively.

Studies of leisure time activities during the depression should be made from this point of view. The efforts of the adult education movement to teach English to the foreign-born, to remove the stigma of adult illiteracy, and to enable the unskilled to learn useful trades has always been handicapped by the fact that those who most needed these educational opportunities had the least time to take advantage of them. With the coming of shorter hours during the depression, this old obstacle to self-improvement was no longer a serious handicap and the time seemed ripe for progress in this direction. It is important to know whether there was any marked tendency during this period toward the use of free time for such purposes.

The declining incomes and restricted budgets characteristic of this period made this a peculiarly appropriate time for emphasis upon leisure time activities of this nature. To what extent was free time used to provide supplementary income for the individual or family? Was leisure looked upon as an opportunity to secure occasional jobs in late afternoons or evenings? Was an effort made to save expenditures by sharing the burdens of household work and giving time to necessary repairs and improvements about the house? Was there a tendency to make use of the new leisure in such a way as to prevent a marked decline in accustomed standards of living?

Any marked developments of this kind are of great significance for they indicate the growth of new attitudes toward recreation and leisure time diversions. The American tendency to identify recreation with pleasure and amusement must give way to a conception of recreation broad enough to include other constructive and useful activities. Relaxation and recuperation may be attained through change from one type of work to another as well as through games and sports. The depression, with its deterrent effects upon many fields of amusement, should have been a favorable time for experimenting with new values in the field of recreation.

The suggestions made in the preceding pages of this chapter concerning types of studies essential for a better understanding of the more important changes in recreational habits and fashions during the depression may be summarized in the following list of research projects:

1. Effects of the depression upon mass recreation
2. Recent changes in the balance between active and passive forms of recreation
3. Trends in informal, unorganized forms of recreation
4. Emphasis upon the constructive use of leisure as, for example, for self-improvement and civic welfare

The study of the effects of the depression upon mass recreation can be approached from different angles, since recreation of this type includes a wide variety of activities. Mass recreation provided under public auspices, as for example that which is available through public parks, playgrounds, and bathing beaches, can be studied with the aid of materials secured from the National Recreation Association and Federal Emergency Relief agencies. An excellent beginning in quantitative research in this field can be made through the use of the data presented in the yearbook numbers of *Recreation* (formerly *The Playground*), a monthly publication of the National Recreation Association. In these yearbook numbers which began in 1910, and which were preceded by bound *Proceedings and Year Book* beginning in 1907, mass recreational statistics are presented for diverse and varying numbers of cities. These statistics in the main relate to community recreational activities conducted under leadership and to facilities used primarily for active recreation.

In the more recent yearbook numbers (beginning with 1928),

these statistics include the name of the city; the population; maintaining authority; number of paid workers; number of volunteers; expenditures for the fiscal year (subdivided by buildings and permanent equipment, upkeep, supplies and incidentals, and salaries and wages); source of financial support; source of information; playgrounds under leadership (classified by portions of year during which they are conducted); the total average daily attendance at playgrounds; number of and total yearly or seasonal attendance at indoor community centers; community houses; playstreets; swimming pools; bathing beaches; golf courses; summer camps; tennis courts; athletic fields; and baseball fields.

Although these data do not possess uniform validity and must be interpreted accordingly, they make possible time series studies of the various activities reported for periods of various length preceding the depression, as well as for the depression years. It should be possible, for example, to select a sample of cities which have submitted reports on one or more activities to the Association continuously, or almost so, for a period of years and to study the trends in selected activities for the period prior to as well as during the depression. Moreover, it should be possible to classify these cities by size, state, or regions in the United States to get at differentials.

In the study of recreation under the President's Research Committee on Social Trends (1930-1931), the data from the National Recreation Association's yearbooks on public playgrounds were presented in tables giving (1) the number of cities reporting public playgrounds by geographical divisions and classes of cities, 1910, 1920, 1930; (2) the number of public playgrounds by geographical divisions and classes of cities, 1910, 1920, 1930; (3) the per cent distribution of playgrounds and urban population by classes of cities, 1910, 1920, 1930; and (4) the per cent distribution of playgrounds and urban population by geographical divisions, 1910, 1920, 1930. By extending these compilations through the years 1931-35, it will be possible to note any significant changes during the depression in providing public recreational facilities of this kind.

In making use of these data, it must of course be kept in mind that the editors of the yearbooks are not in a position to check the accuracy of the reports sent in from the different cities. These annual reports to the Association are not ordinarily official but are sent in voluntarily and may vary in accuracy and completeness from year to year depending upon the reporting authority. But even if the data in the *Recreation* yearbook numbers present too many discrepancies and too many gratuitous estimates to be used as they stand, they provide a framework for further study. One finds, for example, that the numbers reported as attending supervised bathing beaches in Detroit dropped 50 per cent between 1927 and 1933, whereas many other large cities showed an apparent increase. By corresponding with appropriate authorities in these cities, one should be able to obtain the information needed for evaluating and explaining reported increases and decreases. The main value of the year book figures may consist in locating those cities from which, by further work, some sort of continuing statistical series may be eventually constructed, going back to predepression years. *The Financial Statistics of States* and *The Financial Statistics of Cities* issued by the Bureau of the Census can be used to provide an additional check on some of these points.

Time series data of this type might well lend itself to comparison with various economic indexes and may reveal the effects of previous depressions as well as of the last one. Furthermore, such data could also be related to the contributions of the Federal Emergency Relief and Work Programs to the field of mass recreation during the last depression period. It should also be possible to conduct studies of the same character for individual local communities which may or may not have contributed information to the yearbooks of the National Recreation Association. Such local studies may have the advantage of making possible a more detailed analysis of trends in specific types of mass recreation than can be made from the National Recreation Association data.

Similar studies may be possible of other types of activities as well. It should be feasible, for example, to study trends in the development of museums and art galleries, zoölogical gardens and aquariums, libraries and music organizations.[2] There are available sources of data for such studies and these sources can be supplemented by collecting and analyzing recent annual reports of such organizations or obtaining schedule information covering the depression period. In cases in which time series have been established by other investigators, it may be practical to match the sample previously used and collect data for the depression years to determine depression effects. This might be done for museums, for example, on the basis of information available in the *Directory of American Museums,* the *Handbook of American Museums* and the data in the section on "Recent Progress and Condition of Museums" in the *Biennial Survey of Education in the United States, 1928-30,* Washington, Government Printing Office, 1932.

These studies of forms of mass recreation that are provided under public auspices must of course be supplemented by similar studies of those types of commercial recreation that are designed to reach large numbers of people. Suggestions for the study of mass recreation facilities which have been developed on a commercial basis (professional sports, movies, etc.) may be found in Chapter VI where recreation is discussed as a business enterprise.

Among the research projects enumerated above, the one dealing with recent trends in informal, unorganized forms of recrea-

---

[2] The effects of the depression on the use of libraries and on the expenditure of leisure time in reading are discussed in a separate monograph in this series: Waples, Douglas. *Research Memorandum on Social Aspects of Reading in the Depression.*

tion presents perhaps the most difficulties to the student because of the lack of accurate and comparable data. These informal ways of spending leisure do not lend themselves easily to measurement and are frequently too commonplace to be recorded or long remembered. Activities subject to the whim of each individual and dissociated from organizations or institutions are elusive and resist all efforts of the investigator to study them en masse. Obviously, only detailed records kept by individuals of their own daily leisure time activities can furnish the information essential for an analysis of this field of leisure.

Detailed individual records of the kind needed may take the form either of questionnaires or of diaries. The study made by the National Recreation Association in 1934 of *The Leisure Hours of 5,000 People* used a questionnaire which contained a list of 94 free time activities, 37 home and 57 outside activities with instructions to those cooperating in the study to check those in which they participated either occasionally or often. This method has the advantage of reducing to a minimum the work of the collaborators but is not likely to cover the widely varying activities of all classes of people unless very general categories are used. Moreover, a general scheme of classification will not make possible an adequate picture of the ways in which leisure is actually spent.

In a recent study of Westchester County, New York (*Leisure: A Suburban Study* by George A. Lundberg and Others. New York: Columbia University Press, 1934) questionnaires and schedules of various kinds were supplemented by diaries from 2,460 people who recorded their actual daily activities for periods ranging from one to seven days. Care was taken to secure diaries from individuals representing different social and economic groups and to have them scattered as far as possible throughout the different seasons of the year. It is quite apparent that the task of keeping a diary is more laborious than checking a questionnaire, and therefore diaries may prove to be highly selected returns not at all representative of all the people in a given community. A very considerable proportion of the people are not sufficiently literate to keep a leisure time diary accurately or in a manner that could be readily used by the investigator. Those willing to keep a diary are likely to be the most intelligent and civic-minded. There are the further difficulties of inaccurate recording through faulty memories and also unwillingness to set down activities which may come under the ban of social disapproval. The study referred to[3] contains an excellent statement of the problems involved in securing records of this nature and the methods used.

Despite their limitations, data of this kind are indispensable in studies of the large bulk of our leisure spent in activities not connected with organized groups. If there were greater recognition of the need and value of such materials, there could be gradually accumulated a vast amount of data that would throw light on the problems of leisure. The use of this technique is especially appropriate in local community studies and in intensive studies of specific groups, as for example, high school children, unskilled laborers, and housewives.

Another recent study which has investigated informal as well as organized types of recreation is *Middletown in Transition*[4] The authors made extensive use of interview materials, recorded "as literally as possible immediately after the interview." The reliability of such data might be questioned, but the method may be the best one adaptable to certain types of situations.

Since these daily records of leisure can deal only with the present, our knowledge of the depression period must be secured, if at all, from data collected at that time. Fortunately, the data presented in the three studies mentioned above, *The Leisure Hours of 5,000 People, Leisure, a Suburban Study,* and *Middletown in Transition* were collected during the depression and

---

[3] See Chapter 4 and methodological note in the Appendix.

[4] Lynd, Robert S. and Helen M. *Middletown in Transition.* New York: Harcourt Brace & Co. 1937. Chapter VII

therefore form a basis, although fragmentary, for comparison with similar postdepression investigations. The Lynds' study, moreover, can be compared with their earlier work, *Middletown*.[5] It is doubtful whether existing data will make possible anything more than the most general statements concerning changes in the unorganized and miscellaneous groups of leisure time pursuits during the depression. A beginning, however, can be made by using existing data, and as more leisure time schedules and diaries are collected from groups representing all classes of society, this field of recreation can be more adequately charted and understood.

---

[5] Lynd, Robert S. and Helen M. *Middletown*. New York: Harcourt Brace & Co. 1929

Chapter IV

Recreational Facilities Under Governmental Auspices[1]

FOUR or five decades ago when social and civic workers took their first steps toward community action in the field of recreation, the indifference of the public greatly limited the scope of their activities. At the beginning of the public recreation movement private leadership was at the helm and little encouragement was given to those who sought the active cooperation of public authorities. The first playgrounds for the use of the general public were conducted by private agencies and financed by private funds. It soon became apparent that private philanthropy could never bear the burden of widely extended recreational facilities and vigorous efforts were made to bring about municipal support.

During the two decades, 1910 to 1930, rapid progress was made in developing public recreation as a governmental function and municipal appropriations in increasing amounts were made to expand park acreage and construct athletic fields, swimming pools, bathing beaches, tennis courts, golf courses, and other recreational features. County governments and especially those located in metropolitan regions swung into line and established county parks in outlying areas, thus supplementing in a very useful way the city park facilities. The growing interest

---

[1] See also monographs in this series: White, R. Clyde and Mary K. *Research Memorandum on Social Aspects of Relief Policies in the Depression* and Chapin, F. Stuart and Queen, Stuart A. *Research Memorandum on Social Work in the Depression.*

in outdoor life called attention to the recreational possibilities of state and national parks and forests, and led to efforts to make these government lands more accessible and attractive to tourists. During the 1920's remarkable progress was made by the federal government and by some of the states in building up these out-door recreational facilities, and their use grew at a rapid rate.

This modern conception of the rôle of the government in the field of recreation departs widely from past traditions and has had to make its way in the face of much opposition. The accept-ance of governmental responsibility for provision of public recreational facilities involves serious problems of administra-tion and finance which are not easy of solution. Even during the rising tide of business prosperity, adequate appropriations for this new governmental function were difficult to secure. With the coming of hard times during the depression years it was to be expected that one of the first economies in governmental ex-penditures would be a radical reduction in recreational budgets.

The unprecedented drain upon city and county funds during the first years of the depression brought about a marked decline in local appropriations for the administration of public recrea-tion services. According to reports made to the National Recrea-tional Association by 795 cities, the county and city budgets for public recreation in 1933 were only a little more than half the amount appropriated in 1929.[2] This drastic cut, which includes the expenditures of park departments and commissions, recrea-tion departments and commissions, and the recreational activi-ties of school boards, meant in a few cases temporary suspension of recreational services, but, in general, ways and means were found whereby programs and activities could be continued in a more or less restricted manner. Salaries were cut, some of the personnel were discharged, building operations were stopped, and every possible economy was practiced. The experience of the

[2] Weir, L. H. "Parks and Recreation." *What the Depression Has Done to Cities.* Chicago: The International City Managers' Association. 1935. Chapter 5

past few years made it quite clear that public recreation is still regarded in many places as a luxury to be dispensed with during periods of financial stringency.

Fortunately, the decline in local appropriations to recreation departments during the depression was largely offset in many cities by the use of federal and state relief funds for the employment of persons upon recreational projects. In fact, one of the significant developments in the field of public recreation during the past few years was the active leadership and cooperation of unemployment relief agencies in the promotion of local community recreational programs. Never before were relief activities geared so effectively on such a large scale with the recreational needs of communities. One reason for this expansion of the scope of relief work so as to include leisure time activities was the desire to provide employment for so-called white collar workers on relief rolls. Another objective was to build up the morale of the unemployed and overcome as far as possible the deteriorating effects of enforced idleness. This broad conception of the relief problem grew out of the past experience of private social work agencies, and gains its significance during the depression because of its adoption by the federal government as an integral part of its nationwide program of unemployment relief.

Under the leadership of the Federal Emergency Relief Administration and later of the Works Progress Administration, widely extended efforts were made to improve public recreational facilities in rural communities as well as in cities, and to provide leisure time programs not merely for the unemployed but for all who desired to participate. In the promotion of this work the federal government endeavored to cooperate with local agencies interested in public recreation, and to develop sufficient local interest in the enterprise so that it would continue to function when the emergency aid of the federal government was withdrawn. In some cases land suitable for outdoor sports, playgrounds, and camp sites was selected and developed through the labor of the unemployed assigned to work on relief projects. In other places, efforts were confined to building up leisure time programs in which the leaders were as far as possible drawn from among the unemployed who had experience or facility in undertakings of this kind.[3] In a large number of instances the recreational projects of the relief administration were the first energetic efforts to provide wholesome and attractive leisure time activities for the people. This was especially the case in rural and small town communities where leadership and financial support for such undertakings had hitherto been lacking. Some idea of the nature and extent of these emergency recreational activities can be gained from the following statement concerning the work of the Recreation Department of the Works Progress Administration of Indiana[4]

One hundred and ninety-four school buildings have been used for recreational purposes from one to six nights a week during the year. One hundred and fifty-six agencies, churches, libraries, etc., twelve city halls, three court houses, five armories, and fifty-two vacant buildings have been used as recreational centers. In other words, four hundred and thirty-two buildings have been supplied by the people of forty counties for recreational centers. Communities are seeing the value of using public buildings to capacity as well as making use of vacant buildings which have been standing as monuments to the depression. . . . Attendance of the public in all types of recreational activities sponsored by the Department in the state during the past six months has been slightly over one million per month. Of this amount about seventy-five per cent has been in physical activities. . . . Community programs, including Hallowe'en and Christmas celebrations, not only attracted the largest attendance but provided opportunities for local talent. Cultural activities have included sixty-nine choral groups, forty-one bands and orchestras, and ninety-two dramatic clubs. . . . State and local hobby and craft exhibits have attracted much attention. The value of this activity cannot be overestimated. . . . The number of contacts per paid leader has varied from 1,400 to 3,000 per month.

---

[3] Baker, Jacob. "Nation-wide Recreation," *Recreation.* 29:249ff, 1935
[4] "Proceedings of First Annual Meeting of the State Recreation Committee of the Works Progress Administration of Indiana." Indianapolis. 1935. Pp. 16-17 Mimeo.

Throughout the entire country more than 20,000 work projects were completed in the field of public recreation. Every state shared in this recreational program which was sufficiently broad and flexible to meet the needs of different kinds of communities. Among the facilities constructed or improved were stadia, community centers, swimming pools, wading pools, summer camp sites, trails, hostels, orchestra and band shells, and state, county, and city parks. Many vacant lots were cleared for use as temporary playgrounds. This recreational construction work provided jobs for unemployed architects, draftsmen, engineers, mechanics, artisans, and unskilled laborers, while the promotion and development of recreational programs gave employment on a work relief basis to playground directors, instructors in sports, leaders of boys' and girls' clubs, supervisors of camps, instructors in handicrafts, directors of cultural activities, etc. Even those most critical of government expenditures for work relief could not make out a strong case against these recreational projects, for they did not compete with private industry and made permanent contributions to better living.

This recognition by the federal government of the importance of leisure time programs, at a time when public resources were strained to the utmost to relieve the destitute, stands out as a landmark in the history of the public recreation movement. Through the work of the Federal Emergency Relief Administration and the Works Progress Administration the construction of public recreation facilities was pushed forward at least a decade and public interest in wholesome leisure time programs was greatly stimulated. The record of this federal leadership and assistance is available in summary form in occasional bulletins and published reports but the detailed accounts of what actually happened are buried for the most part in unpublished materials in the files of government agencies. Studies of this experience in the promotion of public recreation during the depression would throw much light not only on the field of community organization for leisure but upon problems of cooperation of local governmental units with the federal administration.

The remarkable emphasis upon outdoor recreation during the 1920's was reflected in the growing interest of such federal agencies as the National Park Service and the National Forest Service in the recreational use of the public lands under their control. It was during the decade following the World War that travel through the national parks and forests began to be facilitated by the extensive building of roads and trails, and accommodations for visitors came to be looked upon as an essential part of the responsibility of the government in its administration of such areas. The expansion of pleasure travel during this period advanced in an unprecedented manner, and governmental appropriations were inadequate to keep pace with the demand for improved highways and camping facilities. While the preservation of unique scenery and the conservation of forests still remained as prominent motives for the acquisition of these specially designated governmental areas, their recreational use was given greater importance in federal administrative policy.

With the coming of the depression this program of improvement of park and forest lands was greatly accelerated by the availability of emergency work relief funds. Especially notable was the progress made in the development of recreational areas through the work of the Civilian Conservation Corps. Approximately 150,000 young men in the CCC camps were engaged in this work under the National Park Service with 6000 professionally and technically trained persons to plan and supervise their activities. Trails and roads were constructed, clearing and landscaping were undertaken, camp sites were prepared, necessary buildings were erected, and other work needed to facilitate the recreational use of public lands was carried forward. During 1935, one hundred and eighteen CCC camps were located in national parks, and four hundred and eighty-two were established in state parks in various sections of the country. An important feature of their work was the development of recreational demonstration areas for the purpose of providing adequate camping facilities within reach of large cities. These camp units included tents and cabins, a central lodge or recreation building, a common kitchen and mess hall, and a fireplace for social gatherings. Since the establishment of the first national park more than 60 years ago, probably no other period saw such an advance in the development of outlying areas for recreational use as was brought about during the years 1934 and 1935.

Another aspect of this national public recreation program has been the plan of the federal government to acquire submarginal agricultural land and reallocate to recreational uses those areas most suitable for this purpose. In 1934 five million dollars were set aside by the Federal Surplus Relief Corporation to acquire recreational areas of this type, and the National Park Service was asked to take charge of this part of the federal program.[5] The plans that have been developed in connection with this new experiment in land use are far-reaching and will, if fully carried out, result in greatly expanding government facilities in the field of public recreation. One part of the plan contemplates the establishment of a few regional recreational areas consisting of from 10,000 to 15,000 acres and so located that they may be used by large numbers of visitors. In addition to these large areas it is planned to secure smaller tracts of 1,500 to 2,000 acres in close proximity to large industrial centers, and to develop them as family and children's camps for use by people belonging to the lower income groups. A third type of recreational area is to consist of wayside tracts of 20 to 50 acres situated along principal highways and equipped as picnic grounds for people seeking a day's outing away from the crowded city. According to the *Annual Report of the Secretary of the Interior* for the year 1935, there were approved for acquisition and development 22

---

[5] *Annual Report of the Secretary of the Interior.* 1934. P. 172

projects which will furnish recreational facilities for more than 20 million people living within a radius of 50 miles from large cities. These projects cover more than 340,000 acres and, when completed, will have required an expenditure of approximately $2,800,000.

It is readily apparent that this effort of the government to acquire, on a large scale, submarginal agricultural lands and to equip them for use as parks and playgrounds is an undertaking that breaks with past precedent and involves administrative problems difficult of solution. This new policy of the federal government is an outgrowth of the depression and has been brought forward as an emergency measure without full opportunity to study its many implications and to secure basic data necessary to plan wisely for its further development. Here is a field of investigation of great importance that needs to be exploited with a minimum of delay. How great is the need for outlying recreational areas in different parts of the country? It has been suggested that an area equal to that occupied by urban developments should be accessible for public recreational facilities within 100 miles of each large city.[6] Should this be accepted as adequate provision for this purpose? By what means can we arrive at an accurate estimate of this need? Can submarginal agricultural land be developed into recreational areas without excessive costs? What is a reasonable expenditure of the government for this purpose? What types of recreational facilities are most needed? What kinds of submarginal agricultural lands are best adapted for recreational development? Should such recreational areas be administered by the federal or local governments? What provision can be made for the maintenance of such recreational areas without placing a heavy financial burden upon the government? There is urgent need for careful studies of these and similar questions before the government embarks on an

[6] *Report of National Resources Board.* December 1, 1934. Washington: U. S. Government Printing Office. 1935. P. 146

extensive scale upon the further development of projects of this nature.

Of great significance for the further development of outdoor recreational facilities on a nationwide scale was the inclusion in the first report of the National Resources Board of a section on national and state parks and related recreational activities.[7] This report on recreation prepared by the National Park Service makes available the first official estimate of the recreational land requirements for the entire country. The fundamental problems that must be faced in formulating a national recreation policy are clearly stated in this report. Topography, climate, varying densities of population, differences in occupations and standards of living, public control over private recreational developments, the proper rôle of city, county, state, and federal governments in the recreational field and the effective coordination of their activities stand out as factors that must be given careful consideration, if the problems of public recreation are to be approached in a statesmanlike manner. This official recognition of recreation as a major problem to be dealt with in planning for the future development of the nation's resources came about in connection with the new emphasis upon social and economic planning during the depression, and represents a great step forward in the history of the public recreation movement.

The growing interest of the federal government during recent years in expanding the nation's recreational resources appears also in the fact that at the Twentieth National Recreation Congress held in Washington in 1934, special reports were made by representatives of the National Park Service, National Forest Service, Office of Education, the Children's Bureau, the Agricultural Extension Service, the Federal Emergency Administration, the Subsistence Homestead Corporation, the Tennessee Valley Authority, the Biological Survey, and the National Resources

[7] *Report of the National Resources Board.* December 1, 1934. Washington: U. S. Government Printing Office. 1935. Pp. 144-147

Board. A study of the recreational interests and activities of these various branches of the federal government and the problem of the correlation of their recreational programs is a field of research to which greater attention should be given.

The expanding work of the National Forest Service affords an excellent example of the increasing emphasis on outdoor recreational problems. Established originally as a part of the policy of conservation of our timber lands, the national forests, now comprising approximately 170 million acres, have grown in popular favor as places for outdoor recreation. In response to this interest in their recreational use, the Forest Service has built roads and trails in order to make these forests more accessible, and has undertaken the development of wilderness areas, roadside areas, campsite areas, residence areas, and outing areas to meet the varied recreational needs of vacationists. The wide use that is being made of these facilities is shown by the fact that in 1934, in spite of the decline in pleasure travel during the depression, 38 million people visited or passed through the national forests and 13 millions stayed long enough to enjoy real recreation.[8] These visitors to the national forests occupied summer homes, lodged at hotels and resorts, stayed at camps operated by municipalities and youth service organizations, camped independently at campsites equipped by the Forest Service, and through the use of these living accommodations were able to enjoy the advantages of a vacation in isolated forest areas.

There can be no doubt of the genuine interest of the National Forest Service in the recreational use of the timber lands under their control, but it must be kept in mind that the lumber industry each year makes great inroads upon these forest areas. It is important to know what progress is being made in selective logging which makes possible the economic utilization of the forests without their destruction. What advance is being made in

---

[8] Rutledge, R. H. "Planning the National Forests for Greater Recreational Use." *Recreation.* 29:445, 1935

protection against fire hazards, in reforestation, and in setting aside well located forest areas for permanent recreational use? Are there sections of the country where a more vigorous policy of restriction in the cutting down of timber should be put into effect in order to preserve forests needed for recreational purposes? A thorough study of the whole problem from the point of view of modern recreational requirements, as well as from the standpoint of the lumber industry, should be carried out as a first step in formulating an adequate policy for the future use of the national forests.

This remarkable development of outdoor recreational facilities under the direction of federal authorities has been paralleled by a growing emphasis in many states upon the expansion and improvement of state parks. Between 1933 and 1935 the state park lands of the nation were increased by the addition of four hundred thousand acres.[9] The interest of the state governments in public recreation has been greatly stimulated by the availability of work relief funds for recreational projects, and especially by the assignment of many units of the Civilian Conservation Corps to state parks where they made extensive improvements under the direction of the National Park Service. This cooperation of the federal and state governments in the field of outdoor recreation stands out as a significant byproduct of the depression and raises important questions concerning public recreation policies for the future. How far should the federal government go in the promotion and administration of recreational facilities? What is the proper division of responsibility between the federal and state governments in this field? Should the emphasis in the future be upon the further expansion of national parks and forests or upon state parks and forests? How can coordination of federal and state recreation services be best brought about? These are questions of policy which cannot be

---

[9] Wirth, Conrad. "Outdoor Recreation Planning for America." *Parks and Recreation.* 18:355, 1935

satisfactorily answered without careful studies of recent trends in the development of government lands for recreational use.

Paradoxical as it may seem, public recreation, which with difficulty secured adequate appropriations during prosperous years, made distinct gains during the depression. The financing of recreational projects by federal and state governments in connection with the administration of emergency relief was a factor of great importance in bringing this about. Without this unusual financial assistance, public recreation activities and programs would doubtless have suffered a serious setback because of drastic budget curtailments. We must not lose sight, however, of the existence of other factors during the depression that aided the advance in public recreation. The necessity faced by many people of giving up expensive forms of private recreation led to the crowding of public parks and playfields. The greatly increased leisure made possible by the radical reduction in hours of labor became a news item of wide interest and led to frequent discussions in popular journals of the inadequate facilities for its enjoyment in a profitable and wholesome manner. Furthermore, the staggering amount of unemployment caused social and civic agencies to promote recreational programs as an appropriate means of overcoming the deteriorating effects of long-continued idleness. At a time when the resources of the nation were concentrated upon problems of relief and recovery, public recreation gained in public favor and plans for its further development were made in a more far reaching manner than ever before.

As the conditions prevailing during the depression recede into the background, and, as federal emergency funds are withdrawn, one of the important problems to which attention must be given is the adjustment of public recreational activities to local support. While the federal government will doubtless continue its policy of promoting the recreational use of public lands, local communities must find ways of supporting their recreational programs without further reliance upon federal subsidies. Plans must be made for meeting the cost of operating or maintaining the large numbers of urban recreation areas and facilities that have been developed during the past few years as relief or public works projects. To what extent can they be financed through fees and charges, increased valuations upon benefited properties, or general taxation? One of the experiments made during the depression to lessen the drain upon the public treasury for the support of recreation was the establishment of special fees for the use of certain public recreational facilities. The previous experience with this method of financing municipal golf courses seemed sufficiently successful to justify its wider application during a period when governmental appropriations were at such a low ebb. The considerable number of instances where the policy was adopted of charging fees for the use of public recreational facilities affords an excellent opportunity for an appraisal of this method of increasing revenues. To what extent did the fee system increase the income of recreation departments and what effect did this policy have upon participation by the general public? A study that would bring together the results of the experiments with the fee system during the past few years would be of great use in determining future administrative policies.

In this connection it is also important to know how extensive were the efforts to develop and popularize inexpensive types of recreational opportunities for young people. Some municipal park systems made a special feature of informal dances open to the public at field houses. The formation of hiking clubs was encouraged in some cities and considerable advance was made in the construction of nature trails in outlying parks. The turning of recreational programs and policies in a direction that minimized expenditures of participants stands out as an excellent adjustment to a period of financial stringency. It is important to know the nature of such programs, how the people responded to them, and whether the experiments of this kind were extensive enough to constitute a new trend in the field of public recreation. A study of the reports of park systems during the past few years would throw a great deal of light on this problem.

The public recreational facility that has perhaps made the most rapid advance in public favor since the World War is the municipal bathing beach. This trend apparently continued during the depression for, according to the National Recreation Association, attendance at bathing beaches and swimming pools stands first among all park activities. In view of this increasing interest in water sports, we would expect that among the public works projects of cities, during the depression, there would be special emphasis upon the cleaning up of water fronts and the construction of sewage disposal plants in order to prevent the pollution of streams and lakes. The widespread neglect of this problem in the past has been notorious and it has been difficult to secure local appropriations for this purpose. The availability of federal funds, in the past few years, for local work projects of a kind that would bring about permanent improvements afforded opportunity in many places for the development of facilities for water sports. In some cities considerable progress was made in this direction. A study of the advance made during the depression in projects of this kind and, also, of the work that still remains to be done before urban people can enjoy the recreational use of their waterways should be of special interest to those concerned with the further development of public recreation.

In this rapid review of recent developments in public recreation, that which stands out most prominently is the increased participation of the federal government. The large number of federal agencies engaged in activities pertaining to some phase of recreation gives some idea of the extent of the national forces at work in this field and the varied approaches that are being made to the solution of its problems. Among these agencies are the National Park Service, Bureau of Indian Affairs, Office of

Education, Civilian Conservation Corps, Office of Public Health Education, Bureau of Biological Survey, Bureau of Fisheries, Forest Service, Extension Service of the Department of Agriculture, Bureau of Labor Statistics, Children's Bureau, Resettlement Administration, Division of Recreational Projects and Division of Social Research of the Works Progress Administration, National Resources Committee, National Youth Administration, Planning and Demonstration Services of the Tennessee Valley Authority, and the Housing Division of the Public Works Administration. The recreational projects in which these federal agencies are interested are many and varied. A listing of these projects and study of their contribution to the public recreation movement is a research task which needs to be undertaken. Included in these recreational projects are many surveys of local leisure time facilities and activities and other studies of a similar nature. These studies for the most part have been set up during the past few years as a means of providing work for the unemployed and therefore were subject to serious limitations in the choice of personnel. They have, however, been evidence of the need of studies in this field and have assembled a vast amount of data that should be of great use to the research student.

The preceding paragraphs have presented in broad outline recent changes in public recreation and called attention to some of the problems that are pressing for solution. One of the specific topics discussed above is the large rôle played by federal unemployment relief agencies in the development of public recreation during the depression. A more detailed outline of this particular research problem with suggestions concerning sources and the use that can be made of available materials will now be given in order to illustrate the types of research possible and the kinds of problems encountered in studies in the field of public recreation.

In setting up this research project the approach may be from the point of view of the policies and activities of the various federal agencies or the emphasis may be upon local studies in different communities. The types of problems for which quantitative data should be secured are illustrated in the following list:

I. The cost of leisure time programs to the various types of participating agencies:
   A. Projects financed in whole or in part with Federal Emergency Relief and Work Program funds
   B. Projects of the permanent federal agencies financed out of ordinary budget funds
   C. State contributions
   D. Local contributions
   E. Private agency contributions

II. The allocation of funds expended by these agencies to:
   A. General administration of the programs
   B. Leadership and personnel
   C. Rent
   D. Construction (renovation and new)—types of facilities constructed
   E. Equipment
   F. Types of programs

III. Types of leisure time activities provided:
   A. Recreational
      1. Active forms of recreation (athletic programs, song festivals, parks, etc.)
      2. Passive forms of recreation (concerts, plays, museums, etc.)
   B. Educational
      1. Adult classes
      2. Forums, lectures, etc.
   C. Vocational rehabilitation or retraining
      1. Opportunities for retention of skill
      2. Vocational retraining

IV. Leisure time programs for the unemployed as substitutes for or supplements to "normal" leisure time activity. Comparison and correlation of above data with depression effects on:
   A. Commercial forms of recreation
   B. Trade Schools
   C. School attendance (high school and college, public and private)
   D. Club memberships (athletic clubs, Y M C A, Y W C A, etc.)
   E. Sales of recreation equipment
   F. Indexes of unemployment or relief

V. Attendance at leisure time programs:
   A. Number of participants by type of agency, by type of program

B. Characteristics of participants by type of agency and type of program
  1. Age, sex, color
  2. Occupation and industry
  3. Educational status, etc.

This outline is not intended to be exhaustive, or all inclusive. It merely suggests some of the concrete problems which may profitably be investigated. The official reports and records of public and private agencies can undoubtedly illuminate many, if not all, of these problems. Among the more important sources of data on these problems are the publications and records of such organizations as the National Recreation Association, the Civil Works Administration, the Federal Emergency Relief Administration, the Works Progress Administration, the Public Works Administration, and the Civilian Conservation Corps; the publications of the Bureau of the Census, particularly *The Financial Statistics of Cities* and the *Financial Statistics of States;* the annual reports of the National Park Service and the National Forest Service; and the reports and records of other permanent federal agencies which participated in the emergency relief program.[10] These types of sources[11] can throw light particularly on Problems I, II, III, and IV in the above outline.

The Federal Emergency Relief Administration, the Civil Works Administration, and the Works Progress Administration have a wealth of data relating to their programs. The statistics of the Works Progress Administration, for example, are available [12] for the United States, each state and county and other local areas, on such items as the number of persons employed, earnings and total cost, by types of project. The types of projects identified are the construction and renovation of social and

---

[10] For list of other agencies see *Report on Progress of the Works Program.* Washington, D.C.: Works Progress Administration. December 15, 1936. P. 53

[11] See Chapter I for additional data on source materials.

[12] The Division of Research, Statistics and Records, Works Progress Administration.

recreational public buildings, the construction and renovation of parks and other recreational facilities, library projects, museum projects, recreation projects (leisure time leadership), art projects, music projects, theater projects, and writing projects. Even more detailed classifications than this exist for some of the programs. The scope of the Works Progress Administration program is indicated by the fact that as of September 1936, the estimated approved cost of projects[13] involving parks and other recreational facilities alone had been more than $315,000,000.

It should be possible to conduct local studies in which comparisons are made between Federal Emergency Relief and Work Program contributions to the public recreational movement and "normal" governmental and private recreational activities. Such comparisons can also be related to indexes which measure the extent to which the community was adversely affected by the depression, such as the volume of unemployment, indexes of factory payrolls or employment, or the intensity of relief, depending upon the nature of the statistics available in the community. The Works Progress Administration has on file the FERA monthly data on the total number of cases receiving relief during the course of its program, on a national, state, and county basis in the Division of Research Statistics and Records. It has relief statistics also on the number of families with employable persons, and the number of employable persons, respectively, for the country as a whole, each state, each county, and each city with a population of 100,000 or more in 1930, for the period March 1935.[14] Furthermore the Works Progress Administra-

---

[13] See *Report on Progress of the Works Program*. Washington, D.C.: Works Progress Administration. December 15, 1936. P. 3

[14] See *Workers on Relief in the United States, March, 1935, A Census of Usual Occupations*. Washington, D.C.: Works Progress Administration, Division of Social Research. January, 1937. This is an abridged edition of the data containing selected statistics for the United States and each state. A more complete report is in preparation.

tion has a weekly and a monthly series on the total volume of employment on its Work Program. It also has a census of employable families and persons eligible for the work program as of January 15, 1936.[15] These statistics should serve as fairly good indexes of the severity with which the depression has affected various areas.

Time series studies can probably be made of the adult leisure time programs of some of the private and governmental bodies in this field and may reveal interesting depression and recovery phenomena. Studies of cost should include research into proportionate as well as absolute expenditures. Although it is to be expected that difficulties will be encountered in studies of allocations of funds, particularly if comparative studies are attempted, it seems reasonable to expect to get at least a general description of the kind of expenditures in this field during the depression period. Moreover, so far as facilities and the materials themselves permit, quantitative studies of this type should attempt significant cross classifications of the data. Studies which can include investigation of the recovery as well as the depression period can attempt to gauge the relatively permanent effects of the depression on programs, proportionate expenditures, government participation in the field of leisure time activities, etc.

Finally, where resources permit, it may be possible to collect source materials through schedule studies of representative agencies and groups of persons. Investigations of the schedule type may be the only way of getting data for the study of problem V above—attendance at leisure time programs. It is possible, however, that some of the local offices of governmental and private agencies have attendance statistics. Studies of this prob-

---

[15] *Usual Occupations of Workers Eligible for Works Program Employment in the United States, January 15, 1936.* Washington: Works Progress Administration, Division of Social Research. January 1937

lem should attempt to get at differences in clientele served, between permanent governmental and private leisure time programs, and those provided by federal emergency agencies.

Where comprehensive studies of all or most of these problems are not possible, investigations of the contribution of the federal emergency leisure time programs to specific types of activities would be profitable. Such investigations might include, for example, a description and analysis of federal emergency contributions to libraries and library projects, museums, construction, renovation, or modernization of playgrounds, public recreation buildings, recreational leadership, adult classes, public music projects, public art projects, etc. In this as in the other fields of recreation, the specific character of the research undertaken must necessarily be dependent on local community resources, data, interests, and ingenuity.

In the earlier portions of this chapter other aspects of public recreation were brought out and questions were raised of great importance to the student who seeks to understand the effects of the depression upon the public recreation movement. These questions are summarized below in a brief list of research projects which should challenge the attention of those interested in this field of research. While no attempt will be made here to enumerate the various sources of information, ample data for research purposes are available among the published and unpublished materials of governmental and private agencies. Since much of these data is more or less transitory, it is important that studies should progress with little delay.

1. The use of submarginal agricultural lands for recreational purposes
2. Coordination of recreational activities of federal, state, and local governments
3. Recent experiments in financing public recreation
4. Recent trends in administration of municipal recreation
5. Effect of the depression upon recreation leadership

Chapter V

Community Organization for Leisure

INTEREST in community organization, which reached its high point of development during and immediately following the World War, did not experience a revival during the depression. In the unemployment emergency, local communities turned to state and federal governments for assistance in dealing with their relief problems, with the result that feelings of local responsibility probably declined. Communities accepted without protest this outside invasion of their traditional field of work and seemed little concerned with the resulting effects on local community solidarity.

During the World War there was a similar centralization of federal authority in the interests of effective action, but this proved to be a stimulus to local community activities. While people generally resented the strict regimentation insisted upon by the national government, local communities felt keenly their responsibilities and insisted upon doing their part in carrying on the war work. Communities did not feel submerged by federal control since they regarded themselves as an essential part of the system of national defense. During the War the emphasis was upon their contribution to national need, whereas during the depression the outstanding fact was their reliance upon federal funds.

These entirely different responses of local communities to centralized control during the War and during the depression stand out as interesting phenomena in the field of community organization. While the two situations were so different that the

effects upon communities could hardly have been entirely similar, the extent to which community responsibility broke down
during the depression should be a fruitful theme for study. To
what extent was such a breakdown (where it occurred) the result of the emergency administrative policies adopted by the
federal government? Do federal subsidies necessarily cast a
blight upon local community initiative? In future depressions can
federal assistance be administered in such a way that local cooperation will be developed to a maximum extent?

A study of this kind involves a careful analysis of the steps
taken by the federal and state governments in coming to the
assistance of local communities when the latter found themselves unable to provide the needed emergency relief. The legislation enacted, the administrative policies adopted, the type of
personnel placed in control, the struggle for power among political leaders are all factors of importance in the situation that
developed. Materials of value can be found in the files of administrative agencies, in the reports of field workers, and in interviews with local leaders who occupied important positions
during the emergency.

The bearing of such a study upon community organization for
leisure is readily apparent.[1] Federal subsidies to local communities during the depression were frequently made to projects in
public recreation as a means of providing more opportunities for
employment. In many instances, inadequate municipal appropriations to park and recreation departments were supplemented
by federal grants both for the improvement of facilities and the
promotion of recreational programs. Did the availability of this
federal money increase the tendency of municipalities to evade
their responsibility in public recreation? Was this federal money
spent as wisely and efficiently as local funds? Has this de-
pendence upon outside assistance weakened local interest in sup-

---

[1] See, for example: Lynd, Robert S. and Helen M. *Middletown in Transition.*
New York: Harcourt, Brace and Co. 1937. Chapter VII

port of their own recreational activities? The outcome of this experience during the past few years should be useful in determining administrative policies in the future.

It would be rash, of course, to assume that the general lack of interest in local community organization during the depression was due primarily to too great reliance upon federal subsidies. Other forces also have been at work during recent years which tend to weaken the bonds of local community life. The improvement of highways and the growth of motor transportation have enlarged community boundaries and stimulated new interest in the development of regional organization. Under modern conditions, the range of daily travel has widened, thus making it easily possible to cover distances that formerly would have been entirely impracticable. The recreational community is no longer limited to the neighborhood but extends far beyond the borders of the city. Recreation provided on this wide scale opens up new and more attractive fields and besides can be made available at lower per capita costs.

This trend toward utilization of larger geographical units has apparently been strengthened through our experience in dealing with the many difficult problems of the depression. Local communities were for the most part helpless in stemming the tide of economic distress, for they were facing a situation that demanded cooperative efforts on a wide scale. Public attention was concentrated upon such national undertakings as the National Recovery Administration, the Works Progress Administration, and the new social security legislation. The magnitude of these enterprises captured the imagination of the people and encouraged them to look beyond the local community for leadership in social and economic reforms. A strong impetus was given to the trend toward regionalism with its broader outlook and greater capacity to support extensive undertakings. One of the implications of this expanding horizon was the broadening of the field of urban recreation to include the adjacent hinterland as measured by the outer limits of weekend travel. Both the great advances in methods of transportation and the large spatial requirements of modern forms of recreation seem to make inevitable the use of larger administrative areas in the future development of recreational facilities. Thus far, however, the regional concept has not gone much beyond the planning stage largely because of its conflict with existing governmental units. A careful canvass should be made of the possibility of setting up extragovernmental regional units for the administration of public recreation. The advantages and limitations of developments in this direction should be determined both by actual experiments in different places and by thorough studies of the problems involved.

While the growing interest in regions has already broadened the scope of recreational planning, neighborhoods and local communities still remain the basic units for the organization of leisure. The public recreation movement first developed out of the great need for easily accessible recreational facilities in crowded urban communities, and it has been in municipalities that this movement has made its most spectacular advance. First, under the auspices of philanthropic agencies and later, under the direction and control of the municipality itself, there has grown up our modern system of urban parks and playgrounds with their athletic fields, tennis courts, golf courses, swimming pools, bathing beaches, field houses, and other facilities for leisure time enjoyment. In the development of this municipal recreation program, Park Commissions and Departments, Boards of Education, Playground and Recreation Commissions, Municipal Recreation Committees, Departments of Public Welfare, etc., have participated more or less independently with inadequate coordination of their varied activities. Among the immediate problems pressing for solution are those that grow out of the failure of urban communities to build up any unified administrative control in the field of public recreation. The necessity for economy during the depression made that period an appropriate time to deal with problems of divided authority and overlapping functions. Unfortunately, there was no widespread trend toward unified control of municipal recreation during the past few years, but some significant advances were made in this direction in scattered cities.

One important step toward unification took place in New York City where all park and recreation activities in the five boroughs were consolidated, with a superintendent of recreation for the entire city, working under the direction of one park commissioner. An even more notable administrative advance occurred in Chicago in 1934 when 19 independent park districts were merged into a single park district, thus making possible for the first time in the history of the city unified park planning and development.[2] In some cities attempts were made to prevent overlapping of functions by arranging for the school authorities to accept responsibility for the year-round play activities of children, while the municipality undertook to provide recreation facilities for adults. In other places two or more governmental departments interested in some phase of public recreation brought about coordination of their activities through the employment of a joint executive.

These experiments, however few in number, point the way toward greater economy and efficiency, and are therefore of interest to recreation leaders. Studies of these administrative changes should be made to determine their nature and scope, how they were brought about, and whether they remain in force after the financial emergency is past. It is important to know whether the progress toward more unified control in the field of administration has resulted in higher standards of recreation service as well as in economy of overhead costs. The experience

[2] Weir, L. H. "Parks and Recreation," *What the Depression Has Done to Cities.* Chicago: The International City Managers' Association. 1935. Chapter 5

gained during the depression may prove to be of great value in overcoming the difficulties in the way of more effective co-ordination and control of municipal recreation.

An important problem faced by community organization leaders during the recent financial crisis was the declining financial support of private social agencies and institutions. Community chests with few exceptions were unable to reach their accustomed campaign goals and were compelled to operate with reduced budgets. This breakdown of private philanthropy and the expansion of governmental responsibility for public welfare seemed to usher in a new era in which private social work would play a declining rôle. Especially noticeable were the effects of this new trend upon character building agencies and other leisure time organizations supported by private donations. At a time of expanding leisure for millions of people, many of the social agencies needed to deal with this situation languished because of lack of funds.

This curtailment of activities among organizations of this type seemed, during the depression, to be not merely the result of the financial stringency, but also a natural reaction to the extraordinary growth of government undertakings in the field of social welfare. In the judgment of many people there was developing a definite trend away from the traditional American approach to social problems through the leadership of private agencies. As progress is made, however, toward the restoration of normal business conditions, strong protests are heard against the mounting costs of government, and public opinion is demanding retrenchment in governmental expenditures. The demobilization of governmental emergency agencies may be accompanied by insufficient appropriations to carry on the new recreation projects sponsored by the government, thus making it necessary for private agencies again to come to the front and assume their accustomed place of leadership.

No research could be more timely than a study of the influences that are being brought to bear upon this situation as the more serious effects of the depression disappear from view. Has the public recreation movement been permanently advanced by the emergency relief activities of the government? Is private philanthropy rallying again to the support of leisure time organizations as business conditions improve? What steps are being taken by private social agencies in the field of leisure to adjust themselves to the problems they now face? What will be the future division of responsibility between privately supported and government supported recreation agencies?

One method of studying the effect of the depression upon leisure time organizations supported or aided by private philanthropy, is to analyze the budgets of community chests in a representative group of cities, and to determine whether organizations whose programs fell largely in the field of leisure suffered more serious cuts than did agencies dealing with other types of problems. The organizations of chief importance in such a study would include the youth service associations and those concerned with scouting and related activities. Because of the seriousness of this problem of declining financial support of non-relief agencies during the depression, informal and in some cases extended studies were made by interested groups in a number of cities, the results of which should be available to research students. A canvass of the larger cities will likely bring to light a sufficient number of published and unpublished studies, thus simplifying the task of securing the requisite data. In addition, the National Association of Community Chests and Councils participated in some local studies dealing with this problem and collected data of importance. If a study is made of the kind proposed, it should cover a sufficiently long period following the depression to discover whether private philanthropy rallied again to the support of recreational agencies as business conditions improved. It is too early at the present time to determine accurately the direction of future trends, but a study of the allocation of community chest funds between 1930 and 1937 would throw much light on the problem of financial support of leisure time organizations.

An entirely different group of leisure time organizations includes the wide variety of clubs and associations built up to facilitate the recreational activities of their members and supported by fees and membership dues. It is a matter of common knowledge that many of these organizations were forced during the depression to practise rigid economies and adjust their programs and activities to a declining income. Clubs that had incurred heavy debts in the purchase of grounds and the construction of buildings were in some cases forced into bankruptcy. Large numbers of people gave up their memberships because of inability to continue their payment of dues. In the struggle to meet this situation clubs frequently suspended initiation fees, lowered the annual dues of members, and cut down operating expenses to a minimum. It was quite evident that the pattern of club life developed during the 1920's on a grand scale was ill-adapted to a period of hard times, when extravagant expenditures for recreation were possible only for the well-to-do or wealthy classes.

The large number and wide variety of organizations of this kind make it important to study them in sufficient detail to reveal their varying fortunes during the depression period. Unfortunately, a study of this nature faces serious difficulties in securing data sufficiently representative to be of great value. Golf clubs, tennis clubs, yacht clubs, and other social and athletic clubs are frequently organized independently, and the effort to get facts concerning them becomes an exceedingly time-consuming task. Even those clubs affiliated with a national organization are not likely to report memberships and income to their central headquarters where these data would be easily accessible to students. The most readily available measure of the growth or decline of these clubs and associations is the record of federal taxes paid by clubs having annual dues of $25 or more. According to this source of information, the federal taxes paid by recreational clubs to the Commissioner of Internal Revenue declined more than one-half between 1930 and 1934. While these figures show an enormous loss of income on the part of these clubs and associations, they are too general to be of much value for research purposes. No satisfactory study can be based on these government records since the clubs are not classified in the government reports according to the sports and activities they sponsor, and no differentiation is made on the basis of size of clubs or cost of memberships. If the student desires anything more than changes in total tax receipts from year to year, he must seek his information from other sources. For full data concerning the changing fortunes of these clubs and associations, reliance must be placed upon individual investigations which are both time-consuming and expensive to conduct.

When we turn to the quasi-recreational associations, those that organize leisure for a purpose other than recreation itself, the effect of the depression is less apparent. Luncheon clubs, fraternal orders, civic and improvement clubs, women's clubs, and similar organizations do not impose heavy financial burdens upon their members and, therefore, are not likely to have their status threatened by lack of funds. Their fortunes depend more upon the vitality of their programs and their capacity to adjust to changing situations. The life cycle of such organizations is uncertain and their fortunes rise and fall as fashions in types of organizations change and people's interests are turned in different directions.

A study of the changing status of this general class of organization during the past few years would throw a great deal of light on some of the social effects of this period of hard times. It would be of great interest to know what types of organizations weathered the storms of the depression most successfully, what changes occurred in programs and activities, and what new organizations sprang up to deal with the problems that came to the front. Since no general statistics of these organizations have been centrally collected, their study might well be limited to selected types of organizations fairly representative of the entire group. Information concerning memberships and activities can in the case of federations and national organizations be secured from a central headquarters through bulletins and published and unpublished reports. Basic data showing trends in the development of two types of organizations, luncheon clubs and fraternal orders, were presented in the report of the President's Research Committee on Social Trends.[3] A continuation of these series of tables for the years 1930-1935 would be a suitable place to begin a new investigation in this field.

Data covering the date of founding of each lodge, the number of lodges, and the number of members of the leading fraternal societies can be found in an annual volume entitled *Statistics of Fraternal Societies*. Similar information concerning college fraternities and sororities is published in Baird's *Manual of American College Fraternities*. In the study of fraternal societies, differentiation should be made between those having insurance features and the non-insurance societies, in order to determine which type of organization had greater stability during the depression. The data concerning growth or decline of fraternal societies should be tabulated by geographical divisions, states, and large cities for the purpose of discovering any important variations characteristic of industrial areas, rural regions, and urban centers.

Information concerning the luncheon club movement cannot be secured from any single published source but can be obtained by applying to the headquarters of the various federations. The three federations, Rotary International, Kiwanis International, and Lions International, whose combined member-

[3] Steiner, J. F. *Americans at Play*. New York: McGraw-Hill Book Co. 1933. Pp. 129-132

ship is perhaps more than half of all organizations of this type, publish ample data concerning their development and activities in yearbooks or other official publications, and therefore offer excellent opportunity for intensive study. From the available data curves can be plotted showing the growth by years in the number of member clubs, the number of members of each federation, and the total number of clubs and members of the three federations taken together. Maps may be prepared to show in what geographical areas these luncheons clubs had their greatest or least growth during the depression years. In addition to this analysis of growth, attention should be given to significant changes in the administrative machinery and policies of these organizations. Was there a tendency during the depression for organizations of this type to emphasize centralized control with a loss in local authority and a decline in efforts to adapt programs and activities to local conditions? To what extent did local clubs take on new activities and programs designed to aid in solving problems of unemployment and relief?

If this study of two types of organizations could be enlarged to include a greater variety of associations, it would be possible to come to fairly accurate conclusions concerning the more recent trends that are really significant. A type of organization peculiarly appropriate for study during a period of economic stress, is that connected with the labor movement. In the opinion of some people the new leisure of the working classes has been largely used in promoting and attending meetings designed to increase discontent with existing economic conditions. Advancing leisure from this point of view leads to a strengthening of labor organizations and more insistent demands for changes favorable to the interests of labor groups.

Ordinarily, during a long period of unemployment, labor unions maintain themselves with difficulty and are in no position to pursue aggressive policies. Defections from their ranks occur both because of lack of funds to pay dues and lack of confidence in the union's ability to aid in solving the immediate problems of unemployment. To what extent was this the case during the recent depression? Did the impact of hard times give labor organizations new vitality and a more enthusiastic following? An important trend worthy of careful study is the growing controversy between craft unions, on the one hand, and industrial labor organizations, on the other, which threatens to bring about a complete reorganization of agencies in the labor movement. Of perhaps even greater significance, is the rise of the so-called rank-and-file movement with its dissatisfaction with the more conservative leadership of the past and determination to adopt labor policies more in accord with the wishes of the great mass of working people. In many instances the course of its development seems to have been shaped by the more radical leaders in the field of labor, thus making it the storm center in the conflict between labor and capital. The far-reaching extent of this rank-and-file movement is indicated by the fact that it is not limited to organizations in the field of manual labor, but has invaded also such professional fields as teaching and social work.

These trends in the field of labor have been paralleled by new developments among employers' associations which seem in many cases to have moved in the direction of greater militancy as well as solidarity. A study of these tendencies that have come to the front during the past few years is of great importance as we face the adjustments that must be made in the further struggles between the laboring and employing classes.

Any attempt to study the effects of the depression upon the field of organization should include the rise of new organizations as well as significant changes that took place in those already established. During this difficult period when millions of people faced destitution, public attention was inevitably concentrated upon problems of unemployment and ways and means of dealing with the widespread breakdown of the economic machinery.

In the midst of the many complex factors and forces peculiar to the depression, divided counsels were heard on every hand and there was little agreement about the right course to follow. Reactionary organizations designed to maintain the status quo sprang into existence and gained in power. On the other hand the widely prevailing pessimism concerning the future and the demands for a more secure and efficient economic system gave strength to radical organizations of different kinds. The whole situation was made more confused by the rapid growth of special interest groups organized for the purpose of self-protection with little conception of the larger interests of the people as a whole. The atmosphere of fear and uncertainty characteristic of the worst years of the depression favored the rise of nostrums and cure-alls sponsored by designing or misguided leaders. Townsend clubs, Share-the-Wealth clubs, Unemployed Citizens' leagues, the Silver Shirts, and the Black Legion are examples of types of organizations that flourished during this period. Not all of these organizations spread widely but they made a strong appeal to those whose interests they seemed to promote. During the period of their ascendancy, a large share of the leisure of their constituency was used in enthusiastic support of their policies and programs.

However transient was the life of organizations of these kinds, their rapid growth during a time of advancing leisure raises questions that need to be answered. As these organizations disappear from view, what activities or movements are taking their place? Does the increase of leisure for the mass of the people seem to facilitate the growth of cults and militant, sectarian movements out of sympathy with the traditional social order? What types of organizations seem to flourish during a period of business improvement? With the passing of hard times, do people in general turn their attention in larger measure to play and amusement with less interest in organizations devoted to social and economic reform?

An appraisal of the field of community organization for leisure should include not only the growth and decline of organizations of different types and significant changes in their policies and programs, but also the extent to which the people rallied in support of their activities. In ordinary times recreational clubs, civic and improvement associations, and other leisure time organizations characteristic of American life are largely dominated by those who are well-to-do and possess considerable leisure. Much of the over-organization complained about in many communities means little more than the over-burdening of a small minority of the people who take an active interest in the maintenance of the various clubs and similar organizations. In spite of the multiplicity of leisure time organizations in urban communities, those who spend a great deal of time in meetings or have very active club affiliations are comparatively few in number.[4]

During the depression the reduction in hours of work for large numbers of working people made possible a more widespread participation in organized community activities. On the other hand, insufficient incomes in the case of many people was much more of a deterrent to club life than in ordinary times. It is important to know the effect of these changed conditions upon public support of leisure time organizations. Was there a marked tendency for all classes of people to unite in support of general community affairs? Is there any evidence, for example, of increased participation on the part of the lower economic groups in such civic organizations as parent-teacher associations, federations of women's clubs, men's city clubs, and other well established associations hitherto supported largely by the better educated people with incomes above the averagee? Were the traditional divisions between social classes lessend by common membership in organizations interested in broad questions of

---

[4] See Lundberg, G. A. and Others. *Leisure: A Suburban Study.* New York: Columbia University Press. 1934. Chapter 5

civic welfare, or did the emphasis upon problems of relief and economic unrest tend to increase social stratification in the field of leisure time organization?

In undertaking a study of this nature, it is obvious that figures showing the growth or decline of organizations during the period of the depression are inadequate for this purpose. The important task is to determine possible changes in the clientele of organizations, a factor that is not covered by membership data unless classified by income groups or occupations. Some light, of course, can be thrown upon this problem by a study of the rising or declining fortunes of special interest groups, such as labor organizations, employers associations, unemployed citizens' leagues, and similar organizations whose appeal is primarily to a limited economic class. The important question, however, is to discover whether there was a tendency for the various social and economic groups to join forces in supporting organizations promoting wide community interests.

This problem can be approached best through intensive studies of organizations in individual communities. It should be possible without great difficulty to secure the total number of memberships in a selected group of civic organizations in any given town or city, and from these data there could be computed the average number of affiliations per adult. If this were done for a sufficient number of widely representative cities both large and small, a fairly satisfactory membership index could be established for this type of organization in cities of different size. Through the use of this index, changes in the support of organizations of the type studied could be measured from year to year, and if membership data were secured on a sample basis from the lower income groups, changing trends in their interest in these organizations could also be determined.

One of the difficulties faced by the student is to secure membership data classified by income groups. Since this information is not obtainable from membership lists of organizations, it must be secured either through questionnaires or personal interviews. In this phase of the study of *Middletown,* the investigators used the interview method after having secured their sample of working class families by following up the addresses of shop workers on the payrolls of three leading plants located in different sections of the city.[5] In Lundberg's study of income and club membership in Westcester County, the questionnaire method was adopted, but the tabulation was inadequate for the low income groups.[6]

An even more serious problem is the lack of comparable data for predepression and depression years. The two studies above mentioned give some information concerning the participation of the working classes in organizations in general, but not in sufficient detail for this purpose. Efforts to work out a membership index by income groups for the depression period would not likely be satisfactory because of lack of suitable records and the unreliability of data secured by depending upon the memory of the persons consulted.

In spite of these difficulties, however, it is important to make a substantial beginning in studies of this kind. Reliable data can be obtained for the present situation and a basis can therefore be laid for future studies of changes in participation of community organization activities by the different economic strata in the population.

[5] Lynd, Robert S. and Helen M. *Middletown.* New York: Harcourt, Brace and Co. 1929. P. 507

[6] Lundberg, G. A. and Others. *Leisure: A Suburban Study.* New York: Columbia University Press. 1934. P. 131

Chapter VI

Recreation as a Business Enterprise

NO PHASE of modern recreation presents a more fruitful field for study than its recent growth as a huge business enterprise reaching out in many directions and furnishing employment to large numbers of people. Commercial recreation with its immense investments now ranks as a major industry, securely established, and boasting an annual turnover of several billion dollars. This commercialization of leisure, which owed its first expansion to the increasing demand for various forms of recreation and amusement, has now become a dominant force in the recreational world. So widespread is its influence that our recreational fashions and habits change from day to day in response to the many publicity devices built up by the sports and amusement industries in order to increase their profits. Under the stress of strong competition, extraordinary advances have been made in the expansion of commercialized recreational facilities and activities. The methods of mass production have been utilized in the development of many forms of recreation, thus bringing within the reach of millions of people a much larger variety of ways of enjoying leisure than could otherwise be widely available.

The strong position which commercial recreation occupies in this country is readily apparent from its comparative success in passing through the depression. While drastic cuts in the income of millions of people led inevitably to a decline in their expenditures for amusement and diversions, these economies did not necessitate fundamental changes in methods of providing recreation on a commercial basis. Some fields of commercial recreation suffered more than others, but all seemed to show a remarkable capacity to adjust themselves to a period of retrenchment. Our experience during the past few years makes it clear that the American people do not regard the purchase of commercial recreation as an extravagance to be dispensed with during hard times. Such items as tickets for entertainments and equipment for sports and games tend to be looked upon as necessities rather than as luxuries. Our insistence upon a standard of living that includes reasonable provision for popular leisure time activities made it possible for recreation as a business to continue to show profits in spite of the widespread financial stringency.

A rapid survey of the more easily available evidence concerning recent developments in commercial recreation is sufficient to indicate the varying fortunes of profit-seeking ventures in this field during the past few years. Public support of professional games and sports showed a strong tendency to decline during the depression. Promoters sought to meet this situation by reduced prices of admission, but with the exception of the most important championships the crowds were usually smaller than in former years. In the field of professional baseball, the minor leagues in the small cities suffered most severely. If it had not been for the support of the two major leagues, only the strongest minor circuits could have survived the worst years of the depression. The National League attendance in 1932 fell off 40 per cent from its banner year, 1930, and more than 30 per cent from the year 1931.[1] The American League fared better, but had smaller crowds at its games than during the late 1920's. This decreased support on the part of the public did not extend, however, to the World Series baseball games which, even during the depression, were able to attract capacity crowds in spite of the usual high prices of admission.

---

[1] *Literary Digest:* 114:37. July 30, 1932

Professional football continued to grow in popularity in the small number of cities where it had been established, but it did not spread to smaller cities throughout the country. Popular interest in football, as far as the wider public is concerned, remained limited largely to the college game. Attendance at college football games reached its lowest ebb in 1932, and since then has mounted rapidly, especially on occasions when championships are at stake. Admission prices were, in general, very considerably lowered in the effort to attract the usual crowds. According to an estimate by the Associated Press, attendance at college games in 1935 was 40 per cent greater than in 1932.[2] The trend during the late 1920's toward a less exaggerated emphasis upon football victories continued in a marked manner during the depression, especially in eastern and middle western colleges and universities. In the Far West, the ballyhoo and the commercialism characteristic of this sport in its most popular days showed few signs of abatement in the larger universities able to develop and support winning teams.

Professional tennis was able to carry on profitably during the depression. Each year a professional team toured the large cities of the country and, while their gross receipts were lowest in 1932 and 1933, they continued to be money-making ventures. Professional tennis, in fact, took its greatest strides forward during the depression when Tilden and other wellknown amateur players turned professional. Very possibly, the decision of some of the best American players to abandon their amateur status and use their skill and fame for private profit was a more or less direct outcome of the severe economic pressure of the depression period.

Boxing and prize fighting continued to be a popular sport and several championship matches brought large profits to the promoters and participants. Measured, however, by the federal

---

[2] *All Sports Record Book.* P. 204. 1936

taxes collected on admissions the decline in receipts from boxing contests between 1929 and 1932 was more than 50 per cent.

In the field of commercial amusements, there was also a large
reduction in profits. The theaters, concerts, etc., that were subject to federal taxes may have suffered a loss in patronage of
more than two-thirds between 1929 and 1932. The assessment
of new taxes beginning with 1933 makes it impossible to use this
measure throughout the depression period, but the available
figures seem to show no marked trend toward recovery between
1933 and 1935. It is significant that the establishments classified
by the Commissioner of Internal Revenue as roof gardens and
cabarets did not experience such heavy losses during the first
years of the depression, and in the year 1935 made very substantial gains in income.[3] Apparently, the extravagant expenditures on night clubs were not so seriously curtailed as were the
amounts spent by the general public on less expensive forms of
entertainment.

Attendance at moving picture theaters decreased approximately 40 per cent between 1929 and 1932 and then began to mount
upward. At the end of 1932 more than 30 per cent of the motion
picture theaters were not in use and the construction of new
theaters was practically at a standstill. During the depression,
however, the installation of sound equipment went forward so
vigorously that those equipped to show talking pictures had increased from 9,350 in 1929 to 15,650 in 1933.[4] The loss of patronage of the moving picture theaters was not due entirely to
the depression, but may have been a result also of the diminish-
ing novelty of sound pictures, together with an influx of pictures of mediocre quality. It is significant that while total admissions to theaters declined, there was record-breaking attendance

---

[3] See annual reports of the Commissioner of Internal Revenue, 1929-1935.

[4] Data secured from the *Motion Picture Almanac* for the years 1929 to 1935.
Compare also estimates given in the annual reports of the National Association
of Motion Picture Producers and Distributors of America.

at theaters displaying unusual films which had a wide and popular appeal.

Radio broadcasting weathered the depression perhaps more successfully than any other form of commercial entertainment. The quality of radios and the technique of broadcasting showed marked improvement during this period, while the size of the radio audience continued to grow at a rapid rate. According to the best available estimates, the number of families in the United States owning radio sets increased by 4 million between 1930 and 1932 and made a further gain of 6 million between 1932 and 1935.[5] This extraordinary expansion during a time of business stagnation was brought about by the manufacture of midget sets with lowered prices, as well as by skill and ingenuity in providing popular programs. In spite of the prominence given to advertising in radio broadcasts, there can be no doubt that this form of entertainment has become more securely established in popular favor during the past few years.

Business interests that secure their profits from pleasure travel and the tourist trade suffered serious losses, especially during the first years of the depression. Seasonal hotels, which rely largely upon the patronage of tourists and vacationists, showed a decline of 75 per cent in receipts between 1929 and 1933.[6] The decline in pleasure travel was overcome to a considerable extent by lower fares put into effect by both railway and steamship companies. Largely because of this policy adopted by travel agencies, pleasure travel was one of the first forms of recreation to show a decided upward trend. By the year 1935 travel had increased to the point where transportation agencies were beginning to face the problem of crowded passenger accommodations. In the field of motor touring the American Automobile Association estimated that automobile pleasure travel during

[5] See *Radio in the United States*, a brochure published by the Columbia Broadcasting System in 1936. See *Recent Social Trends*. I:211.

[6] *Census of American Business*: 4:18. 1933

1934 had been restored almost to the 1930 level.[7] An important development in motor touring during the depression was the increased manufacture and use of motor vans and trailers which made possible long vacation trips with minimum expense for food and lodging.[8]

The manufacturers of sporting goods, playground equipment, and other recreation products were forced to reduce their output during the depression. The total value of manufactured articles of this kind was approximately 39 per cent less in 1933 than in 1931. If comparison is made with the year 1927, the dollar value of toys and games, sporting and athletic goods, musical instruments and fireworks, and other recreational equipment was three times greater that year than the total value of such products in 1933.[9] It is quite apparent that the American people economized in their purchases of recreation supplies to a very large degree. It is not likely, however, that there was a corresponding decline in recreational activities because of the widespread tendency during the depression to make far greater use of old equipment than was the case during more prosperous years.

This brief summary is sufficient to indicate the serious financial difficulties faced by recreation as a business enterprise during the past few years. The most striking fact, however, in this survey is not the widespread deflation of the sports industry and the sharp decline in the income from commercial amusements, for such a result was inevitable at a time of general business stagnation. That which is most significant was the extent of the reliance of the general public upon commercial recreation for their leisure time diversions in spite of their decreased purchasing power.

The growing strength and the wide-reaching influence of

---

[7] *Index:* 175-180. August 1934
[8] *Literary Digest:* 120-135, December 18, 1935
[9] *Index:* 167-172. August 1935

profit-making enterprises in the field of recreation make appropriate more detailed studies of the close interrelations of business and recreation and the important rôle of the former in building up patterns and fashions in the recreational world. In such a study, the devices used by commercial recreation interests to sell their wares to the public during the depression may prove to be very revealing. Did they achieve their purpose through a general reduction in prices? Was their bid for popularity made through more sensational forms of entertainment? Was patronage increased through improvement in quality of recreational services, equipment, and programs? Was increased emphasis placed upon radio and newspaper advertising? To what extent were our recreational interests determined by the sports pages of newspapers and the advertising of business firms exploiting some phase of the field of recreation?

All of these questions suggest lines of investigation that may be followed by the research student in the effort to determine to what extent the policies and practices of commercial recreation enterprises were affected by the depression. A computation, for example, of the amount of advertising space purchased in selected newspapers by promoters of commercial amusement and recreation during a given period in the depression, and a comparison of this with a similar computation of space in the same newspapers prior to the depression could be made readily. A similar study of the sports pages of newspapers would also throw light on this problem because of the close interrelations between professional sports and newspaper publicity. In *Americans at Play*,[10] a table was published showing the news space given to athletic sports and amusements in the *Chicago Daily* and *Sunday Tribune* during 1920 and 1930. This table gives the number of column inches devoted to baseball, football, moving pictures, radio broadcasting, total athletic sports, and total

---

[10] Steiner, J. F. *Americans at Play*. New York: McGraw-Hill Book Co. 1933. P. 99

amusements, and is based on a sample comprising the first Sunday and the first Wednesday issues of each month for the two years studied. By extending this table through the years 1931-35, a beginning could be made in determining whether the depression brought about an increase or decrease in the exploitation by the newspaper press of the fields of professional sports and commercial amusements. Wherever files of local papers are available, original studies of this kind may be undertaken and if carried out with sufficient detail will provide data useful in studying recent changes in recreational fashions and interests.

In the field of commercial amusement, the motion picture industry has been the most important development within recent years. During the 1920's its growth was so phenomenal that it became our most popular and most widely accessible form of commercial entertainment. Because of its popularity and low cost of admission, the first onset of the depression did not greatly decrease public patronage and the later decline, although serious, did not necessitate large scale retrenchments. The student interested in following the fortunes of the moving picture industry during the depression can secure the most available figures of attendance at motion picture theaters from the *Film Daily Yearbook,* which has published estimates of weekly attendance for a number of years. While these estimates are perhaps too large, they are widely used by students and very likely reflect fairly accurately changes in attendance from year to year. It is unfortunate that the Commissioner of Internal Revenue does not report separately the federal taxes received from motion picture theaters. If these figures were made available by the federal government, the student would have an additional check upon the rising or declining fortunes of this popular form of entertainment.

Equally, if not more significant than the changes in attendance, are the steps taken by the moving picture industry to stimulate increased popular support. Was there increased production of low quality films that could be exhibited at low prices? Did the industry seek to build up increased patronage through the production of films of unusual merit? It is noteworthy that there have been released during recent years a considerable number of pictures dealing with thrilling feats of science, dramatizing great events in history, and utilizing inspiring music. Have the people become more appreciative of pictures that rank high from an artistic standpoint? A study of the moving picture industry not from the point of view of financial profits, but with an emphasis upon significant changes made during the past few years in the efforts at adjustment to a period of financial stringency would be a research project of wide interest. An approach can be made to a study of this kind through the use of data published by the *Motion Picture Almanac* showing the rapid progress made during the depression in the installation of sound equipment in motion picture theaters in spite of the heavy cost involved. Data are also available describing the nature of the various films released including the cost of production. Through a study of newspaper and magazine comment upon the films shown during the depression years, some idea can be secured of the quality of the films and popular reaction to them. The student, however, must realize that as soon as he turns away from strictly quantitative studies to those that raise questions of social values and involve appraisals of public opinion, research becomes increasingly difficult and may not lead to satisfactory results.

The rapid growth of the radio industry has attracted wide attention, and attempts have been made to determine the increase since 1930 in the number of families owning radios and to secure more reliable information concerning the listening habits of the radio audience. Studies in this field have in a very considerable measure been carried on under the auspices of business organizations interested in advertising and the development of the radio industry, and therefore may be somewhat biased in their conclusions. Among studies of this kind the most important are the Daniel Starch nationwide survey of radio families in 1934 for the Columbia Broadcasting System and the more recent studies by the Joint Committee on Radio Research.[11] The latter include such items as the number and distribution of radio families by states and counties, and analyses of the radio audience by age and sex composition, by income levels, by size of city, and by days of the week. Because of the lack of adequate records these studies made on a comprehensive basis are largely estimates based upon an appraisal of the data that can be brought together for this purpose. The further research needed is a series of studies designed to check the results of these estimates and to provide the most accurate information possible concerning the size and distribution of the radio audience and changes in the listening habits of the people. Perhaps the most useful studies of this kind would be intensive rather than extensive in nature, and limited to small population groups carefully selected so as to be widely representative. Other types of studies that should be made are those concerned with changes in radio programs during the depression. Did the entertainment provided by broadcasting stations improve in quality? What types of radio programs were most popular? Was there a tendency to give greater prominence to advertising? Did educational features have a larger or smaller place on radio programs? A more accurate knowledge of trends in radio programs during the past few years is important in view of the increasing use of the radio as a popular form of entertainment.

An important characteristic of modern recreation is the heavy

---

[11] The Committee includes equal representation from the Association of National Advertisers, the American Association of Advertising Agencies, and the National Association of Broadcasters. Some of the results of these studies have been published in advertising bulletins issued by the Columbia Broadcasting System.

financial outlay that must be made for recreational supplies of various kinds. Every sport and game has its standardized equipment without which participation is impossible. Popular fashion, moreover, has decreed the costume appropriate for each leisure time activity whether it is hiking, hunting, fishing, golfing, skiing, swimming, or horseback riding. The annual expenditures of the American people for recreational supplies and goods of all kinds reached a total of approximately five hundred million dollars in the late 1920's. For the production and distribution of these recreation materials there has grown up the sporting goods industry which now occupies an influential position in the business and industrial world. A study of the declining fortunes of this industry during the depression and the methods used to promote business recovery should be very revealing to the student of recreation. Did sporting goods establishments suffer more from the depression than did those engaged in other lines of business? What types of recreation goods were most affected? To what extent were prices lowered to meet the decreased purchasing power of the people? It is important to know whether a trend has been established during the past few years toward less extragavant expenditures for recreation equipment. Attention should also be paid to the relation between prevailing prices and the costs of production. Are profits excessive in the sporting goods industry? What economies could be brought about that would make possible lower prices for its products? Does the advertising in the sporting goods industry tend to build up habits of extravagance in the purchase and use of recreation goods? This problem of high costs becomes increasingly significant as participation in sports and games spreads more widely among all classes of people. Our experience in dealing with this problem during the depression should be an appropriate starting point for a thorough investigation of the close interrelations between the manufacture and sale of sporting goods and the further development of recreational activities.

During the decade, 1920-1930, the emphasis in American recreation was far more upon outdoor life and competitive sports and games than upon what may be called the café type of entertainment. In the midst of the depression (1933) the eighteenth amendment was repealed by Congress and ratified by states, thus bringing to an end the federal experiment with prohibition. Immediately, beer parlors, cabarets, night clubs, road houses, and similar types of liquor-dispensing places were established in large numbers, and strong efforts were made through advertising and entertainment features to build up patronage and make institutions of these kinds more popular places for the spending of leisure. The large amount of liquor consumption between 1933 and 1935 and the mounting federal tax receipts from cabarets and night clubs furnish some evidence of the growing popularity of forms of entertainment associated with the sale and consumption of liquor. Careful studies should be made in different cities and states to determine whether there is the beginning of a real trend in this direction. Were conditions during the depression favorable for the development of drinking habits? In a period of unemployment and business stagnation is there a tendency to seek relaxation and diversion through drinking and lighter forms of entertainment? The close relation between leisure and drinking is shown by the well-known tendency to consume liquor during weekends and holidays. Is there evidence that the recent expansion of leisure has been accompanied by tendencies to more excessive drinking? Such questions as these cannot easily be answered because of the difficulty of accumulating objective and reliable evidence. It is a matter, however, of sufficient importance to justify a thorough study of all the data that bear upon this problem.[12]

In this connection attention should also be given to the status of professional gambling during the depression. Does gambling

---

[12] See *Middletown in Transition*. Pp. 271-280

tend to increase or decrease during a period of hard times? Apparently, horse racing, which seems inextricably bound up with gambling interests, expanded its sphere of operations during the past few years. It is said that depleted state treasuries caused legislators to seek new sources of revenue by legalizing parimutuel betting at races in states that had formerly resisted all efforts to give horse racing legal status. At any rate, wagers on turf contests are now legal in 21 states whereas during the late 1920's racing was largely concentrated on well-known race tracks located in 6 states. The study of the increase or decline of gambling presents many difficulties because it is frequently carried on under cover and therefore cannot be accurately measured. One approach to this problem has been made possible by the recent wide use of parimutuel betting at horse racing meets, which necessitates the keeping of official records of the amount of money that changes hands through this form of wagering. The large amounts, however, wagered through handbooks and the various gambling devices in use in gambling establishments can be estimated only with the cooperation of those operating enterprises of this kind. From time to time statements concerning trends in gambling appear in the public press or are issued by such organizations as the International Reform Federation, but the figures given are little more than shrewd guesses. In spite of the difficulties involved, it ought to be possible through carefully planned studies to gain more accurate knowledge of changing trends in different forms of gambling during recent years.

The close inter-relation between modern recreation and economic problems stands out most vividly when we view it as a great industry providing a large variety of occupational opportunities to people in many different lines of work. The new uses of leisure have brought new occupations as for example those connected with radio broadcasting and moving picture production. Professional coaches, professional players of games and sports, playground directors, executives and other employees of recreational agencies and organizations, sports writers, the vast army engaged in the field of commercial amusement and entertainment, and the large number employed in the manufacture and sale of recreation goods and supplies are among those who gain a living by participation in recreation as a business enterprise. The remarkable growth of recreational activities during the 1920's expanded the field of employment to a remarkable degree. Attempts to explain the unprecedented unemployment crisis of the past few years must give attention to the far-reaching effects of retrenchments in the various fields of recreation. How extensive was the unemployment caused by economies in leisure time activities? Were recreational jobs during the depression less secure than those in other fields of employment? Does modern recreation tend to build up an industry that can maintain itself satisfactorily only in periods of prosperity? A study of this aspect of recreation is urgently needed as a first step toward building up safeguards against unemployment in future economic crises.

In connection with the research proposed in the preceding pages of this chapter, far more questions have been raised than can be answered with any degree of finality at the present stage of development of recreational research. Many problems of great social significance confront the student of recreation with little possibility of relating them to data at all adequate for their solution. While a similar observation can also be made of other fields of social research, it is peculiarly true of recreation because it is only recently that it has been regarded as a field worthy of serious study. No doubt the rapidly growing interest in leisure-time problems will lead in the future to greater attention to the accumulation of the needed data and also to the improvement of the technique of investigation. In the meantime, the student eager to secure the most fruitful results of his study must concentrate his efforts mainly upon those types of problems for which adequate source materials can be assembled.

In this study of recreation as a business enterprise during the depression, one of the most important problems before us is how to gain a picture of the total quantity of commercial recreation and amusement indulged in by the American public. Did the curtailment of income cause a proportional decrease in amusements bought by the public; did the increase in leisure time cause a rise; or did the two tend to counterbalance each other so that little change took place during the depression? Various ways of getting at this problem have already been suggested, one of the most obvious as well as important being a careful analysis of specific types of recreation. If we can determine the changes that took place in a sufficiently representative number of separate types of commercial recreation and amusement, and then total or average these changes, we should have a fairly adequate picture of the general trend in the consumption of commercial recreation during recent years. In order to indicate the possibility of securing the data needed for this purpose, a brief list of sources of information for various types of commercial recreation activities will be mentioned.[13]

The two major baseball leagues, the American and the National, the American Association of Professional Baseball Clubs, the International League, and the Pacific Coast League can supply accurate information concerning attendance at games of the more important professional clubs. From the annual reports of the State Athletic Commissions, information can be secured concerning gate receipts and attendance at professional boxing and wrestling bouts held in those states that have legalized such contests. Data concerning attendance at professional football games can be obtained from the National Football League. Information concerning attendance at horse racing meets and receipts from parimutuel wagers are available in the reports of State Racing Commissions of 21 states. From the reports of the

---

[13] *Cf.* Vaile, Roland S. *Research Memorandum on Social Aspects of Consumption in the Depression.* Chapter III.

Commissioner of Internal Revenue data can be secured covering the amount of federal taxes paid by roof gardens, cabarets, theaters, concerts, etc. While it is not possible to secure records of attendance at pool and billiard parlors, bowling alleys, dance halls, beer parlors, etc., changes in the number of such places can be determined by consulting the municipal offices where licenses of these establishments are issued. The number of pool and billiard tables is also published in the annual reports of the Commissioner of Internal Revenue. The weekly attendance at moving picture theaters is published in the *Daily Film Yearbook*. Additional data covering other sports and amusements are frequently attainable locally when an intensive recreational study is being made on a community basis. It is quite apparent that this list covers a sufficient number of the major forms of commercialized recreation to make possible dependable estimates of the increase or decrease in the quantity of such recreation during the depression years.

Still another method of estimating changes in the total amount of commercial recreation which may be useful in checking the results of the method just described, is through a study of the changing number of persons employed in recreation and amusement establishments. A change in the total number of employees from year to year signifies three things: first, that business may have increased or decreased so that more or fewer persons were needed; second, that the services rendered per employee increased or decreased so that more or fewer were needed to handle the same amount of business; and third, a combination of the first two.

If, therefore, we have data on the total number of and changes in the number of employees and an index showing the "service rendered per employee," it might be possible to estimate the total quantity of commercial recreation offered the public, and the changes in this amount from year to year. In the following paragraphs, some data giving the total number of employees and a tentative scheme for determining a "service rendered per employee" index will be described.

Data on the number of employees in recreation and amusement is afforded in a publication entitled *National Income in the United States, 1929-1935* prepared in the Division of Economic Research, U. S. Department of Commerce, Washington 1936.

TABLE III

NUMBER OF PERSONS ENGAGED IN RECREATION AND AMUSEMENT, ENTREPRENEURS, AND EMPLOYEES BY TYPE OF AMUSEMENT: UNITED STATES, 1929-1934[a]

CLASSIFICATION	NUMBER PERSONS ENGAGED					
	1929	1930	1931	1932	1933	1934
Total number	232,589	229,771	207,019	177,848	183,160	193,494
Entrepreneurs	33,721	33,602	33,483	33,354	33,225	33,225
Employees, total	198,868	196,169	173,536	144,494	149,935	160,269
Motion picture production	19,602	17,387	16,352	15,224	19,221	21,143
Motion picture theatres . .	129,600	129,600	110,792	86,937	89,011	94,298
Radio broadcasting	9,322	10,128	11,022	11,354	11,000	11,699
Other	40,344	39,054	35,370	30,979	30,703	33,129

[a] Compiled from data contained in Table 200 in *National Income in the United States, 1929-1935*. Division of Economic Research, U.S. Department of Commerce, Washington, D.C., 1936. Sources are discussed in the appendix to that bulletin. There may be quite large errors in the data.

From Table III, enumerating the number of employees in recreation and amusement for the years 1929 to 1934, it is apparent that in 1932, the low point of the depression, about three-fourths as many persons were employed as in 1929. If it is reasonable to suppose that the amount of work, that is, the amount of commercial recreation actually dispensed, which each employee accomplished in 1932 was substantially not below that of 1929, then perhaps the maximum percentage loss in recreational services bought by the public in 1932 was not substantially different from the percentage loss in the number of persons engaged. It is obvious that if the amount of service rendered per employee remained constant throughout the period, then the number of employees at each unit of time (year in this case) would represent the amount of services rendered the public at that time. If the "service rendered per employee" increased during the depression, then it is possible that as much commercial recreation services were bought by the public during the depression as in prosperous times.

According to figures given in the above table, the number of entrepreneurs remained constant throughout the period. This suggests that the number of individual establishments remained fairly constant, again suggesting that the total curtailment in services rendered may not have been very great. It is important that studies should be undertaken which would attempt to determine the changes in "service rendered per employee," and also to determine how the entrepreneur fared, not so much in profits, but from the point of view of establishments successfully remaining open for business.

"Service rendered per employee" can perhaps be studied in the following manner. For the motion picture production industry the number of employees per feature film in each year can be determined. The approximate number of full-time employees is available in the national income publication referred to above and the number of pictures released each year can be obtained from the *Film Daily Yearbook,* which has listed the date of issue of every feature since 1915.

For the motion picture theaters, sample studies can be made in local communities of the number of employees per unit (i.e., per 1,000) attendance. If a number of such studies were made in different sized theaters in different parts of the country, then perhaps an index of "service rendered per theater employee" could be established. Given then the number of employees and the number of patrons served per employee, an estimate of movie attendance can be ascertained.

The Film Daily Yearbook presents the estimated average weekly attendance in United States theaters. If the number of employees varied as the number of patrons, then the number of employees between 1929 and 1934 should each year be a per cent of the 1929 number, equal to the per cent which the attendance is of 1929. The available figures show that attendance declined somewhat more than the number of employees. Both the movie attendance and the employment data should be checked so far as possible, to attempt to explain this difference.

In the field of radio broadcasting the total number of hours broadcast each year for all stations in the United States does not appear to be available. The number of hours broadcast by the Columbia Broadcasting System and the National Broadcasting Company should be readily obtained. If the number of their employees each year is available, then an index of the "service rendered per radio employee" can be ascertained. This index could be expressed as the number of hours broadcasting per employee. Applying this index to the total number employed would give the approximate number of hours broadcast each year.

If sufficient studies along the above line can be made, a composite index of the "service rendered per employee," that is, the amount of commercial recreation actually dispensed per employee, can be made for the country as a whole. Applying this index to the total number of employees in recreation and amusement either as given in *National Income in the United States, 1929-1935* or in other estimates, the changes in the amount of commercial recreation purchased by the public can be estimated.

In a general study of this nature, i.e., where the student attempts to estimate the total amount of commercial recreation served to the American public each year from employment and "service rendered per employee" data, important precautions must be observed. All the data including that of total employment are based on sample studies so that one great source of error lies in the selection of the samples studied. Every effort must be made to see that they are representative to begin with, and that the student understands clearly just what it is that he is studying. When data are available for an entire industry, as for motion picture production, this danger is not as great. But when selected single establishments are studied there is a possibility of serious error. Also, in studying changes on the basis of selected establishments, care must be taken so that the same ones are used throughout. Furthermore, the validity of the data on total number of employees may be questioned. For the purposes of such a study as this, however, the important factor is the comparability of the data from year to year. Published estimates, such as those in Table III, of the total number employed, may be greatly in error; yet the amount of change from one year to another may be quite correct. One of the first things that the student should do is to satisfy himself that the basis for estimating the total employed each year is such as to show correctly the changes which have taken place. It is important also to check the industries studied for possible technological changes which may result in greater "service rendered per employee." Changes of this type may seriously distort the index proposed. Finally, it may be added that a study of this general nature had perhaps best be undertaken by a highly competent research worker in labor problems and attempted on a large and inclusive basis. If local studies are to be made, as for example of a chain of moving picture theaters in a given city, they might all be made along the same pattern so that they can all later be combined.

Chapter VII

Recreation Faces the Future

THE preceding review of the effects of the depression upon the wide fields of recreation reveals something of the stress and strain involved in keeping pace with the onward march of leisure during those difficult years. The widespread necessity for financial retrenchment slowed up the expansion of recreational facilities and forced the majority of the people to practice many economies in their search for amusement and diversion. Some of the varied problems that were an outgrowth of this situation have been set forth in the preceding pages as suitable topics for thorough study and research. The completion of these suggested studies should provide a better understanding of recent recreational trends and throw light on many of the problems of expanding leisure that now confront us.

In this report, which has been concerned primarily with studies dealing with the immediate effects of the depression, there has been little emphasis upon either the ultimate significance of recent recreational trends or the more fundamental problems of policy that grow in importance as recreation becomes one of the major interests of life. The extraordinary expansion of leisure and the insistent demand for more widespread facilities for its enjoyment have led to far-reaching changes in traditional attitudes and well-established customs. In the process of adjustment to the rising tide of recreation, past precedents have been broken and new types of behavior have been built up. As we contemplate the further development of the modern recreational world many challenging problems press upon us.

111

What is the proper balance between labor and leisure? Is it possible to set a final goal in this struggle for shorter hours of work? For many years it was the eight-hour day, but this has long since been outmoded. Can this problem be solved in a satisfactory manner or must it remain a source of perennial conflict? Of fundamental importance also is the proper balance between leisure time activities designed to provide play and amusement and those that are primarily useful. When leisure was merely a brief respite from long hours of exacting toil, it was valued chiefly as a time for rest and for relaxation through pleasurable diversions. As leisure expands, it provides opportunity for self-improvement and public service as well as for sports and games. One of our serious problems is the development of leisure time attitudes and habits that will be satisfactorily adjusted to an era that enjoys long hours of leisure.

Still another question for consideration is the trend toward regimentation and standardization in modern recreation. Under the stress of providing leisure time activities for increasing numbers of people, the methods of mass production tend to be followed. This casts everything into similar molds, leaves little for individual initiative, and ignores differences in tastes and needs. The justification for this standardization is that costs are lowered and recreational activities are made more widely available. Is further advance in this direction possible without causing recreation to become so regimented that its essential spontaneity is lost?

Closely associated with this problem is the proper relation between organized and unorganized leisure time activities. Modern recreation both in the fields of sports and amusements is a product of organization. Team games, commercialized amusements, social clubs, and athletic associations are examples of this modern trend in leisure time diversions. Has our emphasis upon these types of activities forced too much into the background the informal, unorganized ways of spending leisure?

Leisure implies not merely freedom to choose activities, but also freedom from compulsion to follow prescribed routines. How can we prevent the pressure to participate in the many forms of organized recreation from interfering unduly with the enjoyment of leisure in more informal and spontaneous ways?

Questions need to be raised also concerning our popular appraisal of the quality of leisure time activities. Are our widely accepted notions of what is wholesome or unwholesome in recreation scientifically sound or are they emotional judgments growing out of the mores of our times? How can values be measured in the field of recreation? Are recent changes in recreational fashions and attitudes in the interests of human welfare? What kinds of evidence can be produced that will enable us to evaluate present recreational trends?

It is apparent that these general issues and others of a similar nature involve to a large degree differences of judgment and points of view and, therefore, cannot be solved by a simple presentation of arrays of facts. Their study in any systematic way is exceedingly difficult and they may be regarded more as questions for discussion and debate than as specific problems for research. Our best approach to their solution can perhaps be made through a wide variety of studies which contribute more or less directly to a better knowledge of the whole recreational situation. Their solution, however, can never be final since they arise out of the never-ending process of adjustment to changing conditions.

The above considerations indicate some of the limitations of research as a basis for recreational planning. Many of the factors and forces responsible for modern recreational trends are too deeply rooted in our entire social and economic structure to be readily amenable to social control. Such significant developments as the declining opposition to so-called worldly amusements, the widespread use of Sunday as a day of recreation, the approval of women's active participation in athletic sports, the growth of interest in outdoor life, the great expansion of pleasure travel, the extraordinary vogue of competitive sports, the popularity of moving pictures and radio programs, and the almost universal acceptance of recreation as one of the necessities of life for old as well as young, are far more a natural outgrowth of our times than a direct result of foresight and planning in the interests of recreation itself. These recreational fashions and trends have been made possible, if not inevitable, by the expansion of cities, the emancipation of women, the decline of religious intolerance, improvements in standards of living, new developments in transportation, the rise of modern inventions, and various other achievements and events that have come about within recent years.

The dominant patterns in the recreational world are determined by the prevailing mores and respond slowly to efforts of special interest groups to modify them in any essential manner. Recreational planning has been able thus far to do little more than build upon these fundamental patterns and advocate changes that do not depart too widely from generally accepted practices. This limited rôle is of course by no means insignificant, for carefully directed attention to problems of policy and procedure within specific fields of recreation may set in motion changes of great importance. The recent growth of public recreation, which at the outset ran counter to the prevailing mores and traditions, illustrates the possibilities of guidance and control in building up in a more adequate manner leisure time facilities that are felt to be highly desirable.

The rapidly growing efforts to develop a more satisfying recreational world seem to mark the beginning of a new era in which constructive planning will play a much larger rôle than has been the case in the past. The progress that has already been made in this direction has been greatly facilitated by studies designed to provide a sound basis for recreational planning. Further steps toward wisely planned recreational policies are dependent upon our ability to gain a more thorough understanding of the leisure time problems that confront us. Especially do we need to know more about ways in which recreation attitudes and habits are built up. How far is it possible to develop among the mass of the people leisure time interests that would lead to a wise use of leisure? Attention must also be paid to the problem of providing, on a sufficiently wide scale, the recreational opportunities and facilities that would be required if people generally insisted upon spending their leisure in ways that are both satisfying and constructive. As we gain a clearer conception of both the possibilities and limitations of social control in the whole field of leisure and recreation, our efforts to direct recreational trends should become more intelligent and more effective.

Index

Studies in the Social Aspects of the Depression

AN ARNO PRESS/NEW YORK TIMES COLLECTION

Chapin, F. Stuart and Stuart A. Queen.
Research Memorandum on Social Work in the Depression. 1937.

Collins, Selwyn D. and Clark Tibbitts.
Research Memorandum on Social Aspects of Health in the Depression.
1937.

The Educational Policies Commission.
Research Memorandum on Education in the Depression. 1937.

Kincheloe, Samuel C.
Research Memorandum on Religion in the Depression. 1937.

Sanderson, Dwight.
Research Memorandum on Rural Life in the Depression. 1937.

Sellin, Thorsten.
Research Memorandum on Crime in the Depression. 1937.

Steiner, Jesse F.
Research Memorandum on Recreation in the Depression. 1937.

Stouffer, Samuel A. and Paul F. Lazarsfeld.
Research Memorandum on the Family in the Depression. 1937.

Thompson, Warren S.
Research Memorandum on Internal Migration in the Depression. 1937.

Vaile, Roland S.
**Research Memorandum on Social Aspects of Consumption in the
Depression. 1937.**

Waples, Douglas.
Research Memorandum on Social Aspects of Reading in the Depression.
1937.

White, R. Clyde and Mary K. White.
**Research Memorandum on Social Aspects of Relief Policies in the
Depression. 1937.**

Young, Donald.
Research Memorandum on Minority Peoples in the Depression. 1937.